SAMURAI

The World of the Warrior

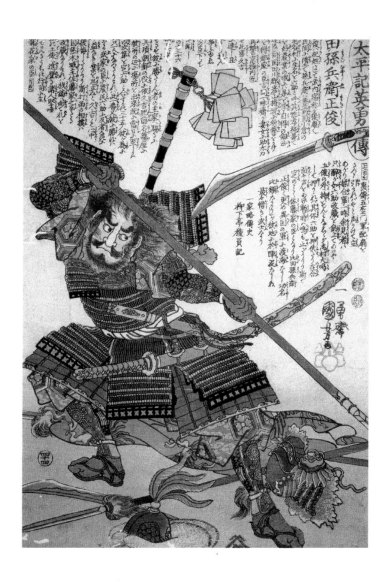

First published in Great Britain in 2003 by Osprey Publishing,
Midland House, West Way, Botley, Oxford OX2 0PH, UK
443 Park Avenue South, New York, NY 10016, USA
Email: info@ospreypublishing.com

This paperback edition first published in 2006.

A CIP catalogue record for this book is available from the
British Library

ISBN 10: 1-84176-951-7
ISBN 13: 978-1-84176-951-6

Editors: Sally Rawlings & Anita Hitchings
Design: Ken Vail Graphic Design, Cambridge, UK
Index by David Worthington
Map by The Map Studio
Originated by Grasmere Digital Imaging, Leeds, UK
Printed and bound in China by Bookbuilders

06 07 08 09 10   10 9 8 7 6 5 4 3 2 1

FOR A CATALOGUE OF ALL BOOKS PUBLISHED BY OSPREY
PLEASE CONTACT:

NORTH AMERICA
Osprey Direct c/o Random House Distribution Center,
400 Hahn Road, Westminster, MD 21157, USA
E-mail: info@ospreydirectusa.com

ALL OTHER REGIONS
Osprey Direct UK, P.O. Box 140, Wellingborough,
Northants, NN8 2FA, UK
E-mail: info@ospreydirect.co.uk

www.ospreypublishing.com

Stephen Turnbull has asserted his right under the Copyright,
Designs and Patents Act, 1988, to be identified as the author
of this work.

Front Cover

Minamoto Yoshiie leads his samurai into action during the so-
called 'Later Three Years War'. (Stephen Turnbull/Japan Archive).

Dedication

To my mother, Joyce Turnbull, on the happy occasion of her
90th birthday, 21 November 2003.

Acknowledgements

I would like to thank everyone who has helped me with this
work, in particular all the institutions that contributed to the
success of my 2003 study tour, from which most of the
accompanying illustrations are taken. I would like to thank in
particular my daughter, Kate, who now provides the
organisation and administrative back-up to my projects.

SAMURAI
The World of the Warrior

CHAPTER ONE

The samurai in a nutshell

This print from Yoshitoshi's 'One Hundred Aspects of the Moon' illustrates the paradox inherent in the world of the warrior. The samurai is playing a *biwa*, the Japanese lute, but he is also fully armed and ready for action. Note the tigerskin cover of his scabbard and the spare bowstring reel attached to it.

The samurai were the legendary warriors of old Japan who led noble and violent lives governed by the demands of honour, personal integrity and loyalty. These ideals found reality in the service the samurai rendered to their feudal lords through government and to their commanders on the battlefield. It was a duty that found its most sublime expression in death.

Yet behind these principles lay an even greater desire than the demands posed by service to another. This was the need to be recognised, because if one reads between the lines in many accounts of samurai bravery the results suggest that loyalty to the group or to the leader had certain limits. In such examples these boundaries were set by a tremendous impulse to be seen not just as a samurai, but *the* samurai, through whose individual actions and prowess the whole world of the warrior might be encapsulated. As the following chapters will show, whatever aspect of his world we explore we will discover a multi-dimensional realm that was constantly under pressure from the competing demands of loyalty and self-expression. At any time in history a resolution had to be sought between the forces of change and the forces of stability. Together they moulded the world of the samurai.

These tensions are most apparent in the historical development of the samurai class. To illustrate these forces at work, and also to provide a chronological framework for the themed chapters that comprise the rest of this book, this chapter will consist of a romp through samurai history, from the origins

LEFT The samurai was essentially a mounted warrior. In this painted screen of the battle of Yashima in 1184 we see samurai of the Minamoto clan. In the foreground, two samurai, one of whom is on foot, wield *naginata*, the Japanese glaives with long curved blades.

of the warrior class to its abolition in the 19th century. In other words, it will be a brief history of the samurai from swords to suits, from top-knots to top hats.

THE ANCESTORS OF THE SAMURAI

Any exploration of the origins of the samurai has to operate along two dimensions. The first is to seek out the evidence for the beginnings of warfare in Japan. The second seeks a link between the use of controlled violence in Japanese society and the use of the word 'samurai' to denote those who were carrying it out.

Even a cursory glance at the evidence shows that there is a huge time gap between the two dimensions. To see the first signs of warfare we have to look towards the first few centuries AD. Although details are sparse about conflict in ancient Japan, the records kept by contemporary Chinese dynasties show a considerable involvement by Japan in the affairs of Korea, where Japanese expeditionary forces took part in the wars between the three rival Korean kingdoms of Paekche, Koguryo and Silla.

RIGHT In this unusual but informative painted scroll we see a group of senior samurai relaxing. One is having a massage, while *sake* (rice wine) is being served to his companions.

This map shows the provinces of
Japan during the Sengoku Period.

The first troops sent abroad by Japan fought only on foot using bows, swords and spears, and in about 400 an infantry army sent from Japan to support Paekche was heavily defeated by a Koguryo army on horseback. Although horses were already being used in Japan as beasts of burden, this battle was Japan's first encounter with cavalry, and the experience must have been a profound one. Within a century of this event there is archaeological evidence of horses being ridden in Japan, and it is not long before we read of mounted warriors heading from Japan for Korea. The reason that Japan was able to mount such expeditions with apparent ease lies in the developments that had been taking place in Japan itself – out of several rival clans in Japan one had emerged triumphant. The name by which the victors are known to history is Yamato, and they are key figures because the Yamato rulers are the ancestors of the Japanese imperial line.

We know very little about the historical processes that took place to give power to the Yamato state, although many pointers have been gleaned from archaeology. Instead the origins of the imperial line are contained in some very colourful legends written down as a series of creation myths when the emperor system had become well established. They are preserved as the *Kojiki* (The Record of Ancient Events) of 712 and the *Nihongi* (The Chronicles of Japan) of 720. These legends of gods and heroes tell us nothing of wars between tribesmen or of one clan dominating the others. Such activities have to be inferred from tales of gods slaying serpents in distant lands. The best-known myth, and the one that is fundamental to understanding the imperial cult, tells how Amaterasu the sun goddess founded the Japanese imperial line when she sent her grandson down from heaven to rule the 'land of luxuriant rice fields'.

Myths aside, the power of these early rulers is vividly illustrated in Japan to this day by the *kofun*, the huge earthen tombs in which they were buried. They date from between the fourth and seventh centuries. They are often keyhole shaped and occupy a huge area of land. Nowadays the *kofun* are covered in trees, and some of the largest imperial tombs are islands in the middle of a lake. Armour, harness, weapons, bronze mirrors and jewels were buried along with the deceased and have been recovered from the very few tombs that have been excavated. On top of the tombs or inside them were placed *haniwa*, primitive but lifelike clay models of soldiers, servants and animals, which may have their origins as substitutes for human sacrifice.

The actual origin of the dominant Yamato line is still a matter of some controversy. Based on the similarities between the grave goods in the *kofun* tombs and contemporary Korean burials, the theory has been advanced that the first Japanese emperors came from Korea, and asserted their superiority in Japan through their use of mounted warfare. This is known as the 'horse-rider theory'. The notion calls into question the uniqueness of the Japanese imperial line, let alone the issue of the first emperors' heavenly ancestors. It has therefore never been popular with Japanese nationalists, and it is interesting to note that as a counter to this idea one of the Yamato creation myths tells of a similar process happening in the opposite direction when Empress Jingo led an invasion of Korea. The story relates how she was pregnant at the time, and on her return gave birth to Emperor Ojin, later deified as Hachiman, the *kami* (god) of war.

Many challenges were made by rival *uji* (the ancient clans) against the dominance assumed by the Yamato rulers. All were ultimately unsuccessful and, by the seventh century, the imperial line felt sufficiently secure to introduce far-reaching legislative changes for Japan. The Taika reforms of 646 were an ambitious set of edicts that sought to curtail any remaining power possessed by the surviving clans by making all of Japan subject to the emperor. One of the first tasks of the reform was to establish Japan's first permanent capital city. This was achieved after a couple of false starts at Nara in 710. Buddhism, introduced to Japan two centuries earlier, flourished in the settled conditions of Nara. The government of Japan, like the design of the capital itself, was modelled on Tang China, and for some time the combination of the two provided a stable society. Any dissatisfied clans, any individuals rebelling against the throne, or trouble from the recently pacified *emishi*, the tribesmen who had been pushed to the north over the centuries, were dealt with efficiently. Kyôto succeeded Nara as the imperial capital of Japan in 894, a position it was to keep until 1868.

It is the means by which war was waged by the Nara and Heian (Kyôto) courts that is most interesting for our story, because the original Chinese model that Japan adopted was of an army conscripted from the peasantry. This proved inadequate to deal with the situations that arose, so instead the government began to grant commissions to make war on local landowners and rewarded them generously for their trouble. So, instead of controlling the clans that had once been its rivals, the government's military needs now encouraged them. Their elite warriors, who rode horses, used bows and were supported by tenants drafted as soldiers, were the forerunners of the samurai.

The ninth century was not kind to Japan. It was a time of economic decline marked by plagues and episodes of starvation. These were factors that led to resentment against the central government which an influential local ruler could exploit to his advantage – when riots, lawlessness and localised opportunistic rebellions plagued Japan there was nowhere else for the court to turn. By the beginning of the tenth century the government was granting far-reaching powers to its provincial governors to levy troops from these skilled fighters, and to act on their own initiative when disorder threatened. Delegated tax collection, family ties to the court, rewards for military service and rivalry over official appointments all helped create a system that favoured the strong and the rich, and saw them grow stronger and richer.

THE FIRST SAMURAI

The tenth century is the time that we first see the term 'samurai', which literally means 'those who serve', being used in a purely military context. At first it referred to men who went up to the capital to provide guard duty. In time it began to denote a military man who served any powerful landlord. The word rapidly acquired a strong aristocratic and hereditary aspect, so that samurai lineages began to be recognised and valued. Some were the descendants of the *uji*. Others were newly established families whose reputations were secured by military prowess and whose glorious pedigrees were just starting to be written. The service that the samurai families rendered to the Heian court made them even more wealthy and powerful, and by the

The two best-known incidents at the battle of Uji in 1180 are illustrated in this print. To the left, three warrior monks from Miidera temple hold back the advancing Taira samurai on the broken beams of the Uji bridge. To the right the defeated commander Minamoto Yorimasa prepares to commit *hara kiri*.

11th century two particularly strong clans had emerged. They were the Taira and the Minamoto, and their exploits were to dominate Japanese politics for the next hundred years.

Samurai from the two families took part on both sides during the Hôgen Rebellion of 1156, an armed encounter in Kyôto that was concerned with the imperial succession. It was not long before another succession dispute put the Taira and the Minamoto into direct opposition. The Taira were victorious in the struggle (the Heiji Rebellion of 1160) and disposed ruthlessly of their rivals. But in 1180 the survivors of the Minamoto purge, key members of whom had been children spared by the Taira, reopened hostilities at the battle of Uji. This was the first armed conflict in a war that was to become known as the Gempei War, from the Chinese reading of their names: 'Gen' for the Minamoto (Genji) and 'Hei' for the Taira (Heike).

The Gempei War is fundamental to understanding samurai history. First, the battles that took place such as Ichi no tani, Yashima and Dan no Ura created benchmarks for samurai excellence that were to last for the whole of samurai history. Heroic tales and works of art logged the incidents in the Gempei War as a verbal and visual catalogue of heroism that would show future generations the most noble, brave and correct ways of being a samurai. Nearly all the factors that were to become indelible parts of samurai culture have a reference point somewhere within the Gempei War. Prowess at archery and hand-to-hand fighting, the juxtaposition of art, poetry and violence, undying loyalty to one's lord and the tremendous tradition of ritual suicide, all have key passages and proof texts in the tales of the Gempei War.

The other way in which the Gempei War made its mark on samurai history lay in the steps the victors took to confirm their triumph. In 1192 Minamoto Yoritomo took the title of shogun. This was the rank that had previously been bestowed temporarily on samurai leaders who had accepted an imperial commission to deal with rebels against the throne. Yoritomo, whose family was now unchallenged in Japan, took the title for himself for his new role as military dictator. The difference was that the temporary imperial commission had now become a permanent one and was not relinquished until another eight centuries had passed and Japan had entered the modern age in 1868. The position of shogun was also made hereditary within the Minamoto family. Government exercised by the shogun was called the *bakufu*, a name derived from the *maku*, the curtains that surrounded a general's headquarters on a battlefield. It was a good choice for a new system of ruling that relegated the emperor to the position of figurehead with immense religious power but no political power. The control of Japan's affairs now lay with the leader of the greatest family of samurai.

CHALLENGES TO THE SAMURAI

The Minamoto did not have long to enjoy their success. Yoritomo was killed in a riding accident in 1199, and their dynasty only lasted two more generations before they were overthrown by the Hôjô. Out of respect for the tradition of the title staying with the Minamoto, the Hôjô rulers styled themselves regents rather than shoguns. It was therefore the Hôjô *shikken* (regency), not the Minamoto *bakufu*, that faced a brief attempt at imperial restoration in 1221. This was speedily dealt with, and another half century was to pass before the Hôjô took the brunt of a very different threat to the survival of Japan itself.

The 13th century in continental Asia was the time of the Mongols. Under the leadership of Genghis Khan and his successors these fierce horsemen had broken out of the steppes and gone on to conquer distant lands, from Korea to Poland. Japan entered their sights in 1274 with a raid on the southern island of Kyûshû. This was followed by a serious attempt at invasion in 1281 that was driven off by a combination of samurai bravery and a knockout blow delivered by the weather. The fateful storm was the famous *kamikaze*, the 'wind of the gods' that destroyed the Mongol fleet as it lay at anchor. The repulse of the Mongols added a further set of reference points to sit alongside the experiences of the Gempei War in the world of the samurai. As late as 1945 the term *kamikaze* still had such a powerful resonance of the destruction of an invader that it was adopted as the name for the suicide pilots who crashed their planes onto American ships.

The next major challenge posed to samurai hegemony during the 14th century came from a further attempt at imperial restoration. This movement, led by the energetic emperor Go Daigo, was ultimately no more successful than the brief venture of 1221. But its execution was more prolonged, and succeeded in adding more names to the pantheon of samurai heroes and more glorious exploits to the litany of the Gempei War and the Mongol invasions. In particular, these Nanbokuchô Wars or 'Wars Between the Courts' (so called because there were for a time two rival emperors) produced one samurai who was to be celebrated for centuries because of his loyalty to the person of the emperor. His name was Kusunoki Masashige. When the imperial line was finally restored during the 19th century he was the exemplar from history who was presented to the loyalist samurai as the ideal they should follow. Sadly for Masashige, his devotion to the imperial cause led to his suicide at the battle of Minatogawa in 1336. The battle was fought against Masashige's advice, and the inevitable defeat that was the result of his obedience to the imperial will required the ultimate sacrifice.

Go Daigo's attempted coup had one other result, because when the Hôjô regents were overthrown the power gap was filled by the Ashikaga family. As they were of Minamoto descent they

Occasionally in Japanese history we come across examples of women warriors. In this print by Yoshitoshi we see one such female samurai putting paid to two assailants who have invaded her home.

re-established the *bakufu* and ruled Japan as shoguns for the next two hundred years. But once again a single ruling family found it impossible to keep under control the numerous volatile and powerful samurai families. The 15th century in Japan is therefore a catalogue of apparently minor clan squabbles settled by force, until one such dispute affected the heart of government itself. This was the tragic Onin War, fought from 1467 to 1476.

LEFT This panel of a print by Kuniyoshi shows *ashigaru* (footsoldiers) of the Takeda family at the fourth battle of Kawanakajima in 1561. They are the retainers of Yamamoto Kansuke, who committed suicide when he realised that his battle plans had gone wrong and that the Takeda were heading for certain defeat. The dramatic background of Mount Fuji heightens the tragedy of the scene, because Kansuke's suicide proved to be unnecessary.

BELOW The fiercest opponents of Oda Nobunaga, the first *daimyo* to begin the process of re-uniting Japan during the Period of Warring States, were the warrior monks of the Ikkô-ikki. In this print we see monks from the Ikkô-ikki headquarters of the Ishiyama Honganji fighting Oda Nobunaga's samurai in the last battle before they were defeated.

When the fighting was over Kyôto was in ruins, the shogun was disgraced and a number of civil wars were taking place elsewhere in Japan.

THE PERIOD OF WARRING STATES

The Onin War ushered in a century and a half of conflict to which historians have given the name the Sengoku Jidai, the Period of Warring States, a term taken from the Chinese histories, although the Japanese wars were between clans and families rather than between states as such. Their leaders called themselves *daimyo*, which literally means 'great names', and 16th-century *daimyo* such as Takeda Shingen, Uesugi Kenshin and Date Masamune were to make 'great names' for themselves that eclipsed anything their heroic ancestors may have achieved during the Gempei War. It was also a time of great developments in samurai warfare. Only the strong survived, and to be strong involved fielding large armies armed with good weapons. The successful *daimyo* had ready access to large numbers of troops by using *ashigaru* (footsoldiers), whom they trained to use bows (once the traditional samurai weapon), long spears, and the newly introduced firearms. Crude Chinese handguns had been known since 1510, but the introduction of European arquebuses in 1543 caused something of a military

Date Masamune (1566–1636) was
one of the greatest *daimyo* of the
Period of Warring States. In spite
of having only one eye he
triumphed in numerous battles in
northern Japan, and only yielded to
the overwhelming force mounted
by Toyotomi Hideyoshi. This
waxwork statue of him appears in
the Date Masamune Historical
Museum in Matsushima. He is
wearing the bullet-proof armour
with which he outfitted all his
troops. His helmet has a lavish,
crescent-moon crest.

revolution. The European traders were the initial source of supply,
but the Japanese soon turned their hands to manufacture and
production. The effective use of the weapons took a little longer
to be realised when the *daimyo* Oda Nobunaga began to use

The interior of the Kanran-tei (literally 'the place for viewing the ripples') at Matsushima. This tea arbour was originally in Fushimi castle in Kyoto, and was given by Toyotomi Hideyoshi to Date Masamune after the latter submitted to him. It now stands on a rocky outcrop overlooking Matsushima Bay.

volley-firing by trained infantry squads. His victory at the battle of Nagashino in 1575 drew heavily on these new techniques.

The major military contests in the Sengoku Jidai were the struggles for power between the most powerful *daimyo*, out of whose ranks there would ultimately be only one winner. Oda Nobunaga (1534–82) was the first *daimyo* to take steps in that direction when he occupied Kyôto and abolished the shogunate in 1568. He died in 1582. The eventual reunifier of Japan turned out to be one of Oda Nobunaga's samurai who had risen through the ranks from his initial position as an *ashigaru*. Toyotomi Hideyoshi (1536–98) had become one of Nobunaga's most trusted generals, and reacted with a mixture of loyalty and opportunism when he heard the news that Oda Nobunaga had been assassinated. In a series of political moves and military campaigns such as the battles of Yamazaki (1582) and Shizugatake (1583), Hideyoshi asserted his authority. Some *daimyo* became his allies after failing to beat him in battle. Tokugawa Ieyasu, who was defeated at the battle of Nagakute in 1584, is the best example of the accommodative approach. Others proved to be more stubborn, and in 1585, in his first campaign off Japan's main island of Honshu, Hideyoshi conquered the island of Shikoku. In 1587 he followed this up by the subjugation of Kyûshû and the mighty Shimazu family, until

Tokugawa Ieyasu (1542–1616) was the final victor in the Period of Warring States. His triumphs at Sekigahara (1600) and Osaka (1615) ensured that the Tokugawa family held the dominant position in Japanese society for the next two and a half centuries.

with the submission of the northern *daimyo* in 1591 Hideyoshi controlled the whole of Japan. His humble origins prevented him from re-establishing the shogunate, but his power was greater than that of any shoguns had ever been.

It was only then that Hideyoshi began to overreach himself with an attempted conquest of China. The invasion of Korea that he launched in 1592 was intended to be the first stage of the plan, but Ming China rose to the challenge and a fierce war began. The combination of the Chinese invasion, the Korean navy with their famous turtle ships and the activities of Korean guerrillas ensured that the Japanese expeditionary force never got further than the Korean peninsula. They were finally and ignominiously driven out in 1598, having achieved nothing other than the devastation of their nearest neighbour.

By the time of the Japanese evacuation Hideyoshi was dead, and the nominal ruler of Japan was now his five-year-old son Hideyori. It was a situation that could not last long in the hotbed of samurai politics. Soon two rival factions emerged: those who were loyal to Hideyori, and those who saw the future in the person of Tokugawa Ieyasu (1542–1616), the one *daimyo* who was powerful enough, and clever enough, to challenge the succession. The two sides met in battle at Sekigahara in 1600. Ieyasu was victorious in one of the most decisive battles in Japanese history. As Ieyasu was of Minamoto descent he was able to become shogun, and Tokugawa shoguns ruled Japan until the mid-19th century. In 1614 there was a brief and very worrying attempt by Hideyori to claim back his inheritance, but this only led to the huge sieges of Osaka conducted in the winter of 1614 and the summer of 1615. Osaka was a total victory for the Tokugawa. The survivors of the sieges were liquidated, and apart from the short-lived Shimabara Rebellion of 1638 no other military challenge threatened the Tokugawa for two more centuries.

THE PASSING OF THE SAMURAI

The means by which the Tokugawa shoguns asserted their authority were many and varied. The shock provided by the Shimabara Rebellion, which had a fanatical Christian element to it, prompted the government to sever all its connections with Europe. There had long been a suspicion that Catholic missionaries were acting as stalking horses for the European powers. They also provided the contacts through which a rebel against the Tokugawa could obtain European weapons. The *bakufu*'s Exclusion Edict of 1639 banned all foreign trade except through carefully controlled outlets. China and Korea remained as trading partners, but the sole contact with Europe for the next 200 years was through a handful of Protestant Dutch merchants who were allowed to reside on the artificial island of Dejima in Nagasaki harbour.

To control any potential rivals at home, the *daimyo* were given responsibilities for ruling their own territories (the *han*) under the overall control of the Tokugawa. It was a system backed up by constant surveillance and by measures such as the Alternate Attendance System. The basis of this was nothing more than a colossal hostage system. The *daimyo* resided in their castle towns while their families lived in Edo, the shogun's capital. The *daimyo* would meet them when they made their annual visit to Edo to pay their respects to the shogun. They were required to march there at the head of a huge army equipped with the finest armour and weapons: a clever ploy designed to keep them as busy and as poor as possible.

This happy state of affairs continued until Western ships began appearing in Japanese waters in the early 19th century. The sightings culminated in the brief appearance of Commodore Perry's US fleet in 1853, followed by his formidable return in 1854. Trade concessions were demanded. Impressed and fearful of the power of the outside world, the Tokugawa government began to sign trading treaties and opened up their ports to foreigners. This aroused much anger among traditionalists in Japanese society, who felt that the shogun was abandoning key Japanese values and allowing himself to be disadvantaged through fear of the 'Western barbarians'.

The main opposition to the shogun's policy of opening up Japan came from *daimyo* such as the Môri of Chôshû and the Shimazu of Satsuma whose ancestors had suffered under the Tokugawa. These critics were equally awed by the military might of the West, but sought to learn new military techniques so that Japan could be defended. Soon two separate aims developed among the traditionalists: the overthrow of the shogunate and the expulsion of foreigners, and the intentions came together in the symbolic figure of the emperor. To the slogan of 'Sonno joi' ('Honour the emperor and expel the barbarians'), the opponents of the Tokugawa sought to replace the shogun by force and to restore power to the emperor. A civil war followed that was fought with great bitterness and devotion on both sides. There had been two failed attempts at imperial restoration in the past, but this third attempt, known as the Meiji Restoration, succeeded completely. A few diehards, such as the loyal samurai of Aizu in northern Japan, fought for the shogun until they were completely crushed by the forces of modernity. In 1868 the last Tokugawa shogun handed back to the new emperor the imperial commission to rule that had been granted to Minamoto Yoritomo in 1192.

Emperor Meiji was restored to a level of political power that the occupant of the role had not enjoyed for centuries, but the outcome of the Meiji Restoration was not the expulsion of the foreigners that its supporters had originally wanted. Instead there was an enthusiastic embracing of Western culture. It was a massive U-turn that most people saw as inevitable. There was also no room for a hereditary warrior class in the new Japan, so a European-style army replaced the sword-wearing samurai. Many of the 'old guard' resented the changes, and there were some flickers of resistance, such as the Satsuma Rebellion of 1877. But apart from such doomed anachronisms Japan stepped squarely onto the modern stage, and the world of the samurai was left behind as a memory that would inspire the nation, terrify its enemies and mystify its allies for many years to come.

CHAPTER TWO

The genuine articles

As the queues at the Tower of London will confirm, no visit to any capital city is complete without seeing the country's crown jewels. Kept safe behind plate glass, they intrigue the thousands of visitors who admire the gold and precious stones that make up a nation's objects of kingship, and marvel at their survival.

Yet out of all the nations that have preserved their regalia of sovereignty, there is one notable exception when it comes to the question of access. No visit to Japan will ever include a trip to see the Japanese crown jewels. One can see, albeit from a great distance, the places where they are kept, but no display of them is ever made. Instead they have lain undisturbed and unseen for well over a thousand years, wrapped in a succession of cloths and boxes. Literally unseen that is, by anyone, even including the man to whom they are ritually presented on his enthronement. No emperor of Japan has seen any item of his own regalia since the 12th century.

Even though they have remained invisible for so long, the imperial regalia have always played an important role in Japanese history. The three items: the mirror, the sword and the jewel, are the objects that were, and still are, the legitimators of kingship: the symbol and guarantee of the eternity of the imperial throne. Writing in the 14th century, Kitabatake Chikafusa said:

Heaven and earth from of old change not; sun and moon alter not their light; still more do the Three Sacred Treasures endure in the world – and that which is eternal is the imperial throne which perpetuates our nation.

In addition to acting as symbols of authority and integrity, the crown jewels were also believed to magically protect their possessor against evil powers. Sometimes these 'evil powers' were manifested in human form as rivals to the imperial line, and on such occasions the regalia played a very different role. As this chapter will show, because the possession of the crown jewels defined the sovereign, the question of legitimacy was theoretically no problem. When there was a succession dispute the mere ownership of the regalia allowed the true emperor to be identified from pretenders to the throne. The matter is, however, complicated by the fact that in early samurai history the regalia that rival imperial candidates vied with each other to possess were not the actual crown jewels, but the officially recognised replicas. Imperial disputes, in such cases, became a matter of identifying the genuine articles, both in human and material terms.

THE FIRST REGALIA

We first encounter a written mention of the Japanese imperial regalia in the creation myths of the Yamato rulers. In the previous chapter a brief reference was made to the story of how Amaterasu, goddess of the sun, sent her grandson to rule the world. An earlier story tells how Amaterasu was so frightened by the behaviour of her brother Susano-ô that she hid in a cave. The world was therefore plunged into darkness and her fellow *kami* tried desperately to entice her out. As a trick, Amaterasu was told that a rival *kami* even more powerful then she had arrived. Then a female *kami* danced a ribald dance outside the cave, and so loud was the merriment that Amaterasu's curiosity got the better of her. She peeped cautiously out of the cave. The first things she saw were a precious jewel hanging from a tree, and next to it the face of her new rival. This made her start, and she was grabbed before she had time to realise that what she was actually looking at was her own reflection in a bronze mirror.

The mirror and the jewel that had restored light to the world became the first two items in the imperial regalia. The third item makes its appearance later in the creation myths. In the province of Izumo lived a fierce serpent with eight heads and tails. The *kami* Susano-ô resolved to destroy the serpent. He began by getting it drunk on *sake* (rice wine) and then hewed off its heads and tails. But as he reached the tail portion his blade was turned, and Susano-ô discovered a sword hidden there. As it was a very fine sword he presented it to his sister Amaterasu, and because the serpent's tail had been covered in black clouds the sword was named Ame no murakomo no tsurugi, the Cloud-Cluster Sword. Amaterasu handed the sacred sword, the mirror and the jewel to her grandson Ninigi when he took possession of the earth. He eventually passed the three items on to his grandson Jimmu, identified as the first emperor of Japan, to whom traditionally are given the dates of 660–585 BC.

The three items were then handed down as the symbols of sovereignty from one emperor to the next, with only the sword being put to any other use. This incident occurs in the legend of Prince Yamato. He was the son of Emperor Keiko, the 12th emperor according to the traditional reckoning, who sent Prince Yamato off on a military campaign. Before leaving for war, Prince Yamato called in at the Grand Shrine of Ise where his aunt was the High Priestess. To arm him for his campaign she gave him the Cloud-Cluster Sword, and Yamato was able to put it to good use when he was ambushed in the province of Sagami.

The Atsuta Shrine in Nagoya, where is kept the sacred sword, one of the three items that make up the Japanese crown jewels. The sword was named Ame no murakomo no tsurugi, the Cloud-Cluster Sword, but renamed the Grass-Mowing Sword when it saved the life of Prince Yamato.

The Sun Goddess Amaterasu was so frightened by the behaviour of her brother Susano-ô that she hid in a cave. The world was therefore plunged into darkness. As a trick Amaterasu was told that a rival *kami* even more powerful then she had arrived. She peeped cautiously out of the cave and she was grabbed before she had time to realise that what she was actually looking at was her own reflection in a bronze mirror. The mirror, shown here on the tree, became the first item in the imperial regalia.

Having fooled him into entering a grassy plain, his enemies set fire to the grass to burn him to death, but Prince Yamato cut through the burning grass and made a path to safety. Thus, the sacred sword acquired a new name: Kusanagi no tsurugi, the Grass-Mowing Sword.

THE SACRED REPLICAS

Prince Yamato had risked the fate of one the three sacred treasures of Japan in his quest for military glory. It is therefore strange to read that long before this incident occurred one of his ancestors had taken steps to safeguard both the regalia and his own sanity by having copies made. The creation and subsequent fate of the sacred replicas adds a fascinating twist to the story of the Japanese crown jewels.

The creation of the replicas of the imperial regalia happened very early in traditional history. The account tells us how Emperor

Sujin, who is supposed to have reigned between 97 and 30 BC according to the legendary chronology:

began to feel uneasy at dwelling on the same couch and under the same roof, beside the mirror sacred to Amaterasu-o-mikami and the Grass-Mowing Divine Sword, and being greatly overwhelmed by their awe-inspiring divine influence he ordered them to be removed to the village of Kasanui in Yamato province where a new holy site was prepared for them.

Even though he was overawed by the magical properties of the three sacred treasures, Emperor Sujin clearly recognised their importance as the defining objects of his sovereignty. He therefore had replicas made of the mirror and sword (there is no mention of the jewel) that were to be kept beside his person just as the genuine articles had been. The text continues:

The new mirror and sword are the identical sacred emblems which the Imbe family offer to the emperor as the divine insignia at his enthronement ceremony which protect the legitimate sovereign against hostile evil powers.

It was not long before the original mirror found a permanent place of enshrinement in the place where it has remained to this day. In the 26th year of his reign, Emperor Suinin, who was the son of Emperor Sujin and succeeded to the throne in 29 BC according to the traditional reckoning, transferred the mirror and the sword to the Grand Shrine of Ise. Suinin was the father of Emperor Keiko and therefore the grandfather of Prince Yamato, who took such risks with the sacred sword. The original sacred sword eventually made its way to the Atsuta Shrine in Nagoya, but the mirror has stayed within the Naiku, the 'inner shrine' of the two great Shintô shrines at Ise.

As may be expected for objects that have acquired such mystical powers, the treatment accorded to the replicas has traditionally been accompanied by the same reverence as that accorded to the originals. For the first 800 years after Emperor

Two items of the Japanese crown jewels, the original jewel and the replica mirror, are housed here in the imperial palace in Tokyo. This building, formerly Edo castle, was the seat of the Tokugawa shoguns and became the imperial palace after the Meiji Restoration in 1868.

Suinin transferred the original mirror and sword to Ise, the replicas of these two objects were physically handed down from emperor to emperor as the undisputed legitimators of their succession and the protectors of the throne. But towards the end of the ninth century a change took place in the procedure. The replica of the mirror was accorded a special place of enshrinement in a building within the enclosure of the imperial palace called the Naishi-dokoro (the Place of Inner Attendance). From this time on it was no longer removed from its sanctuary to lie beside the replica sword and original jewel. Instead the mirror's shrine of concealment became the place where the solemn announcement of the imperial succession was made to Amaterasu. The sword and the jewel were not enshrined, but were kept in a special room in the palace called the Sword and Jewel Room.

None of the three 'practical' regalia, if such an expression may be used, has managed to escape completely unscathed from the ravages of time. Disasters both human and natural have taken their toll. There are 20 recorded instances of the replica mirror, the replica sword and the original jewel being damaged by fires or earthquakes. The mirror was slightly damaged in a fire in 960, while in 1005 another fire totally destroyed its sanctuary, although the mirror was rescued. Not many years later in a fire in 1040 the mirror was so badly damaged by the heat that only a portion of it was left, and that was badly mutilated. Such was the reverence for Emperor Sujin, however, that no repair was ever made. The profanity of repair, it was believed, would be less acceptable than leaving it in what must be a very sorry state.

THE REGALIA GO TO WAR

Ravages caused by the hand of man began with the Gempei War of 1180–85. This was the civil war fought between the Taira and Minamoto families that eventually resulted in the Minamoto leader supplanting not only the Taira but also the emperor by becoming Japan's first shogun. But, while the war was still raging, the sacred link between the emperor and the crown jewels was of vital importance in determining the righteousness or otherwise of the causes and interests espoused by the rival sides. Patterns of loyalty were given added complication because of the practice whereby reigning emperors would abdicate in favour of a pliant relative and continue to rule behind the scenes as 'cloistered emperors'. So in 1180 the first battle of Uji came about because of a succession dispute between Prince Mochihito, the second son of Cloistered Emperor Go-Shirakawa and the reigning Emperor Antoku. Mochihito's cause was supported by the Minamoto. The Taira supported Antoku, whose grandfather was Kiyomori, the leader of the Taira.

The Minamoto were heavily defeated at the battle of Uji, but there were other young leaders waiting in the wings, and by 1184 the positions occupied by the two clans was beginning to be reversed. The Taira were first driven from their base at Ichi no tani on the coast of the Inland Sea near to present-day Kobe, by a daring rear attack led by the celebrated general Minamoto Yoshitsune. They withdrew to the island of Yashima just off the shore of Japan's third main island of Shikoku. Here another desperate fight took place, but for the second time the Minamoto were not able to complete their victory. That was accomplished the following year, when the Minamoto moved against the Taira base at the extreme tip of Honshu. A decisive battle took place in the narrow straits of Shimonoseki that divide Honshu from

A waxwork in the Heike Monogatari Museum in Takamatsu depicting the battle of Ichi no tani in 1184. These life-sized models convey a dramatic impression of the mounted charge down a steep slope that was led by the celebrated general Minamoto Yoshitsune. Yoshitsune is holding a bow in his left hand. To his right rides his faithful companion the warrior-monk Benkei.

Kyûshû at a place called Dan no Ura. The nearby island of Hikoshima was the Taira's last refuge, so it is not surprising to hear of them pulling back to this place and taking with them the sacred person of the Emperor Antoku, now eight years old. He had with him the three items of imperial regalia that proved he was genuine. What is surprising to read is that both the child emperor and the regalia were actually taken into battle.

Dan no Ura was a sea battle, fought in the style of the times, with the samurai conducting a battle more as if it was being fought on land than on the sea. It was also the most decisive battle in Japanese history. When the Minamoto ships went into action a long-range archery duel began. The Taira took the initiative in the early stages because the tide conditions were in their favour and their commander Taira Tomomori, who was a good seaman, used his experience and knowledge of the tidal conditions in the strait. At the start of the battle there was an ebb tide flowing slowly into the Inland Sea, so the Taira ships

A painted hanging scroll of the battle of Dan no Ura in the museum of the Akamagu Shrine in Shimonoseki. The Taira flagship is shown as a large and ornate vessel. The child emperor was not kept on this ship but on another.

attempted to surround the Minamoto fleet. By 11.00 am the two fleets were closely engaged with sword and dagger fighting, but at about this time the tide changed, and began to flow westwards out of the strait. This gave the advantage to the Minamoto, who exploited it to the full. Gradually the battle turned in their favour, and victory was assured when Miura Yoshizumi, one of the Taira allies, turned traitor and attacked the Taira from the rear. He was also able to inform the Minamoto that the largest ship in the fleet did not contain the emperor, so the Minamoto turned their forces to the correct target. The Minamoto archers first concentrated their fire on the rowers and the helmsmen, and the Taira ships were soon out of control and began to drift back with the tide. All seemed lost, and there was only one course of action available to keep the emperor and the regalia from falling into Minamoto hands:

Then the Nii Dono (Antoku's grandmother), who had already resolved what she would do, donning a double outer dress of dark grey mourning colour, and tucking up the long skirts of her glossy silk hakama, put the Sacred Jewel under her arm, and the Sacred Sword in her girdle, and taking the Emperor in her arms, spoke thus …

The epic *Heike Monogatari* continues with a moving speech by the imperial grandmother, at the end of which she takes the

When the battle of Dan no Ura in 1185 was known to be lost, the imperial grandmother took the child emperor in her arms and with the words, 'In the depths of the ocean we have a capital', sank with him beneath the waves. The replica sacred sword was also lost. This is a waxwork of Dan no Ura in the Heike Monogatari Museum in Takamatsu.

child emperor in her arms and with the words, 'In the depths of the ocean we have a capital', sank with him beneath the waves. A few minutes later the replica mirror almost joined them:

Dainagon no suke had been just about to leap into the waves with the casket containing the Sacred Mirror when an arrow pinned the skirt of her hakama to the side of the ship and she stumbled and fell, whereupon the Genji soldiers seized her and held her back. Then one of them wrenched off the lock of the casket to open it, when suddenly his eyes were darkened and blood poured from his nose. At this Taira Dainagon Tokitada no Kyo, who had been captured alive and was standing nearby, exclaimed, 'Hold! That is the Holy Naishi Dokoro, the Sacred Mirror that no profane eye must behold!' Whereat the soldiers were awe-stricken and trembled with fear.

Realising that the battle was lost, many of the Taira committed suicide by jumping into the sea. Some weighed themselves down with anchors, while one used two Minamoto samurai as weights to hold him under the water.

Now the whole sea was red with the banners and insignia that they tore off and cut away ... while the white breakers that rolled up on the beach were dyed a scarlet colour.

The sight of the sea at Dan no Ura turning red from the dye of the Taira flags and the blood of the slain warriors is one of the most powerful images to come down to us from samurai history.

This photograph illustrates three epic moments in samurai history described in this book. It is the site of the decisive battle of Dan no Ura in 1185, but in the distance is the promontory on which stood Moji castle, the scene of one of the first actions in Japan involving cannon fire. Finally, it was along these straits that a joint Western fleet bombarded the forts of the Chôshû *han* in 1863.

The so-called Heike crabs who live in the vicinity of the site of the battle of Dan no Ura have shells that have the appearance of the face of a dead samurai.

One other image from Dan no Ura is of the so-called Heike crabs of the area, whose shells have the appearance of the face of a dead samurai. But the unique feature of Dan no Ura was the loss in battle of the replica sacred sword. The original jewel was recovered, and the replica mirror provided its own defence mechanism as we have seen, but the replica sword was lost for ever. As Heike Monogatari puts it so simply:

At the Hour of the Rat the Sacred Mirror and the Sacred Gem were handed over to the keeping of the Daijiokwan. The Sacred Sword was lost, but the Sacred Gem in its casket floated on the waves and was recovered by Kataoka no Taro Tsuneharu.

The appendix to *Heike Monogatari*, known as *The Book of Swords*, gives further details about the loss of the sword:

Greatly grieving that what had been preserved from such ancient days should now be lost in this generation, they procured divers to search for it, but skilled as they were they could not find it. This was because the Dragon King had taken it and laid it up in his palace beneath the waves.

For the brief period from 1190 to 1210 a sword called Hi no omashi no goken 'the Sword of the Imperial Day Room', a weapon provided from the imperial collection, was used in the enthronement rites. But early in the reign of Emperor Go Tsuchimikado a priest of the Grand Shrine of Ise received a revelation from Amaterasu to the effect that a sword from the Ise Treasure House should be set aside for the enthronement ceremonies. Beginning with the year 1210, and right down the succeeding centuries, all new emperors have made use of this sword.

GENUINE FAKES

Little more than a century was to pass before Japan was once again plunged into crisis by the attempt at imperial restoration by Emperor Go Daigo. For over half a century Japan had two rival emperors: those from the Northern Court, who lived in the imperial palace in Kyôto, and the Southern Court, based in exile in Yoshino, deep in the mountains of present-day Nara prefecture. Once again the imperial regalia had a crucial role to play in determining the legitimacy of the claimants and swaying the allegiance of their supporters, but matters were never as simple as they had been at the time of the battle of Dan no Ura. There was first the question of who owned the original imperial regalia. Then there was the problem of the sacred replicas that acted in a practical role, to which of course had been added in 1210 the sacred replacement for the replica sword. And then things started to get really complicated!

The regalia played a role right from the start. When his mission to overthrow the shogunate became known to his rivals in 1331, Go Daigo fled from Kyôto:

Then they drew forth a carriage, set the imperial regalia inside, and trailed silken garments from beneath the inner curtain as though a court lady sat within.

Go Daigo escaped with the regalia to Mount Kasagi, the first of several mountainous refuges that were to conceal him over the next few years. He was assisted by samurai such as the great loyalist Kusunoki Masashige and Nitta Yoshisada. But in particular one other supporter of Go Daigo now concerns us.

This was Ashikaga Takauji, who, after rendering loyal service, proved to be disobedient to his sovereign's wishes. Nitta Yoshisada was sent to deal with him, but Takauji defeated him and marched against Kyôto. After a brief success Takauji was driven away, but returned to defeat Kusunoki Masashige at the battle of Minatogawa in 1336.

The death of his most loyal general at the hands of Ashikaga Takauji prompted Go Daigo to flee to the mountains again. As before he took the imperial regalia with him, but this time he had apparently left behind a set of copies of the replicas, which Ashikaga Takauji proceeded to use in the enthronement ceremony he arranged for the nominee of the Northern Court, Emperor Komyo. From that time on the Southern Court argued for their legitimacy on the grounds that they had the genuine replicas while the Northern Court had only fake replicas!

Go Daigo died in exile in Yoshino in 1338. By this time Ashikaga Takauji had been appointed shogun by Emperor Komyo, but still the Southern Court fought on, sustained by a younger generation of Kusunoki family members. The most notable samurai in this regard was Masashige's son, Masatsura, who perished at the battle of Shijô-Nawate in 1348. Resistance from the Southern Court officially ended in 1383, and in 1392, under the good offices of Shogun Ashikaga Yoshimitsu, the two imperial lines were reunited. Unfortunately, the agreement that Yoshimitsu had brokered whereby the succession would alternate between the Northern and Southern lines was never put into effect. The last Southern emperor, Go Kameyama (1383–92), kept his part of the agreement by returning the regalia to Kyoto at the time of reunification. But Go Komatsu, the Northern emperor who succeeded Go Kameyama, abdicated in 1412 in favour of his son, Shoko, and when Shoko died another Northern emperor succeeded him. So the imperial succession remained with the Northern line, where it has stayed until the present day.

THE LAST FLOURISH

Although the Nanbokuchô Wars had supposedly come to an end with the return of the regalia to Kyôto and the happy accession of just one emperor, isolated supporters of the Southern Court felt aggrieved that the succession had stayed with the Northern line. They first argued that Prince Ogura, the son of Emperor Go Kameyama, should have taken the throne instead of Emperor Shoko. When the prince died they continued to support his successors, and created trouble for many years to come, using the imperial regalia in the most dramatic fashion since Dan no Ura.

Kitabatake Mitsumasa conducted their first revolt. He fought on behalf of Prince Ogura in 1413, but was quickly crushed in battle. Kitabatake Mitsumasa planned a further revolt when the Northern emperor Go Hanazono took the throne in 1428. This time the plot hinged on an attempt to assassinate Shogun Ashikaga Yoshinori, but the conspiracy was discovered. A third and final attempt took place in 1443. The Northern Court was then in some disarray because Shogun Ashikaga Yoshinori had actually been murdered in 1441. The Akamatsu family had carried out the murder for reasons totally unconnected with imperial legitimacy. Taking advantage of the fortunate confusion, Kusunoki Masahide, a descendant of the great Kusunoki Masashige, launched a surprise attack on the imperial palace in the name of Prince Manjuji, the current heir to the Southern line. During the raid he took care to steal the imperial regalia and made off with them and the prince to the protection of the warrior monks of Mount Hiei. They were hotly pursued by samurai from the Ashikaga shogunate, and on being defeated Prince Manjuji took his own life.

The replica mirror and the sword were regained, but Kusunoki Masahide escaped with the jewel and Prince Manjuji's two sons. Just like his illustrious ancestor he based himself in the mountains of Yoshino. There the elder of the two sons, Prince Kitayama, was proclaimed emperor, and his younger brother was given the title of shogun. Buoyed up by the legitimacy endowed on them by the possession of at least one of the crown jewels, this bizarre remnant of the Southern Court resisted all attempts to shift them for another 11 years.

Their denouement came in 1457 when a group of samurai from the Akamatsu family made their way through the wild Yoshino mountains to the Southern emperor's makeshift palace deep in a river valley near the village of Kotochi. They presented themselves as sympathisers to the cause, and attracted little

The battle of Shijô-Nawate in 1348 was one of the fiercest encounters of the Nanbokuchô Wars. Kusunoki Masatsura, son of the great Kusunoki Masashige, was defeated along with his companions in one of the last serious attempts at resistance by the Southern Court. This print depicts the action that has become known as the 'Last Stand of the Kusunoki Family'.

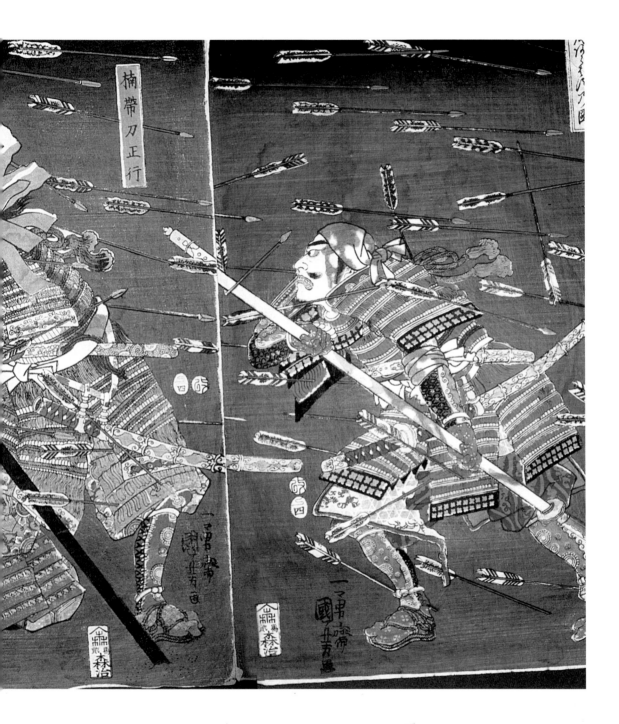

suspicion because the Akamatsu family had been involved in the murder of Shogun Ashikaga Yoshinori in 1441. But the reality of the situation was that as a way of regaining his favour the Akamatsu had promised the new shogun that they would destroy the Southern Court.

The interlopers struck under cover of a heavy fall of snow. One group attacked the imperial palace while the others assaulted the headquarters of the 'Southern shogun' a few miles away. The emperor defended himself bravely but was cut down and killed. The assassins escaped with his head and the sacred jewel, but the snow was so deep that they were unable to cross the Obagamine Pass before night fell. So they buried the emperor's head in the snow and rested for the night. The following day they were attacked by local villagers, who drove them off, leaving the emperor's head behind. Its location was revealed when blood seeped through the snow, but that was the only treasure they recovered. The sacred jewel was returned to Kyôto and has stayed with the regalia ever since.

THE ETERNAL REGALIA

During the Onin War of 1467–77 the Yamana family briefly displayed a so-called Southern emperor to try and counter the blatant manipulation of the real emperor by their rivals the Hosokawa. But there was no one willing to fight for him, and from this time onwards pretenders to the imperial throne disappear from Japanese history. The great trio of unifiers: Oda Nobunaga, Toyotomi Hideyoshi and Tokugawa Ieyasu, had no need for imperial nominees bearing crown jewels. Their legitimacy to rule came out of the barrel of a gun.

Yet there is one strange footnote to the story. In 1945 no less than 17 men who objected to Emperor Hirohito's surrender appeared from nowhere as 'pretenders to the throne'. They all claimed to be the rightful emperor who knew Japan's true destiny. One of them, a shopkeeper from Nagoya called Kumazawa Kando, even came to the attention of General Douglas MacArthur. He stated that he was descended from the Southern Court, and therefore had greater authority than Emperor Hirohito to decide whether Japan should capitulate or not.

Tokugawa Ieyasu needed neither pretender to the throne nor crown jewels to achieve power. Here we see him in command at the battle of Sekigahara in 1600, on a painted screen held in the Watanabe Museum, Tottori.

As for the imperial regalia, the replica mirror and the original jewel made an epic journey from Kyôto to Tokyo in 1868. When Emperor Meiji was enthroned it was decided to transfer Japan's capital to the city (then called Edo) that had been the shogun's capital since 1603. They are housed within the imperial palace in Tokyo. The original mirror is still in the Ise Naiku, while the original Grass-Mowing Sword lies in the Atsuta Shrine in Nagoya. The sacred replica sword, of course, still lies at the bottom of the sea off Dan no Ura, if it has not yet completely rusted away.

So the precious items still exist, even though they are still unseen by anyone. As the appendix to *Heike Monogatari* reminds us, this makes Japan very special. The following passage refers to the jewel, but the sentiments apply to all three items of Japan's crown jewels and their turbulent history:

And this casket is never opened, so that no one has seen what is in it. The Emperor Go Reizei-in, for some reason or other tried to open the casket, but when he took off the lid immediately a white cloud rose from within it … Japan is a small country, but in this matter it surpasses even great ones. If the emperor himself, lord of the mightiest powers, was not permitted to see it, how should ordinary people do so, much less any others of lesser rank still?

CHAPTER THREE

A passion for ancestors

The Ii family in action at Osaka in 1615 is the theme of this painted screen in Hikone Castle Museum. Having fired their arquebuses the *ashigaru* have shouldered their weapons and now run along beside the bulk of the cavalry and the large number of other foot-soldiers carrying the red banners. Some of the samurai are mounted while many others are charging along on foot. Their *sashimono* bear their names in gold.

In Gilbert and Sullivan's *The Mikado*, that well-loved operetta set in Japan but where all the jokes are about England, Pooh Bah claims a pedigree so astonishingly complete that he can trace his descent from 'a single protoplasmal primordial atomic globule'. This was almost the only aspect of Japanese culture that Gilbert got right, because the value attached to pedigree and lineage is a vital aspect of the world of the samurai. The heavenly lineage of the Yamato rulers and their imperial descendants has already been noted, but a similar pride burned within the breast of every samurai warrior, even if his lineage could be traced neither to a divine ancestor nor even an atomic globule.

PEDIGREE AND THE RITUALISATION OF COMBAT

This passion for ancestors was expressed within samurai culture by several mechanisms. The most dramatic ways appear in the early war chronicles when a samurai challenges a worthy opponent to single combat. In that situation the tradition developed whereby the challenger would recite the names of his ancestors and their illustrious exploits, finishing, naturally enough, with his own. The samurai to whom the challenge had been issued was then expected to respond with his own family history, at the end of which battle would be joined.

The pride that a samurai expressed by reciting his ancestral pedigree had several strands to it. The first was the straightforward factor of the reverence given to one's ancestors within Japanese religious belief. Ancestor veneration derives from the centrality of the family, rather than the individual, in the Japanese religious world, and is a mechanism whereby dead family members are enabled to continue playing a part in the world of the living. To a samurai, therefore, the illustrious ancestors who had founded his lineage continued to have an influence and a relationship with the present. Every year, at the time of the Bon Festival, the ancestral spirits would be welcomed back into the household. At other times they would be remembered where they were enshrined. We referred earlier to the great Shintô shrines of Ise and Atsuta, but the imperial ancestors are not the only ones to have been enshrined as *kami*. Heroes, ancestors and tragic figures are among the thousands of enshrined deities remembered in the numerous Shintô shrines dotted all over Japan.

For a samurai, however, an ancestor was not merely someone you honoured because of religious obligations. The ancestor was the person from whom the samurai was descended and from whom he had received his family name. The ancestor had therefore established the samurai's own elite status and also given him something to which he could aspire when he entered battle. Thus it was that the first stage in the complex ritual surrounding combat involved bringing these ancestors into action through the proclamation of the warrior's pedigree.

Works such as *Hôgen Monogatari* and *Heike Monogatari* contain several examples of pedigree proclamations, of which the most illuminating illustration concerns two separate proclamations delivered on different battlefields but concerning the same ancestor. The actual exploit that was related with such pride occurred during the so-called Later Three Years' War of 1083–87. A certain samurai called Kamakura Kagemasa, who was only 16 years old, was fighting at the stockade of Kanazawa when he received an arrow in his right eye. It appears to have gone clean through his eye socket, because the shaft buried itself in one of the plates of his helmet. Undaunted, the young hero broke off the arrow and immediately loosed a shaft of his own, killing his assailant. In an amusing conclusion to the story, we read how, during a lull in the fighting, one of Kagemasa's comrades attempted to remove the broken arrow and found that he would need to place his foot on Kagemasa's face if he was

This detail from a copy of the picture scroll of the Gosannen War probably shows the incident when Kamakura Kagemasa received an arrow in his right eye. It appears to have gone clean through his eye socket, because the shaft buried itself in one of the plates of his helmet. This tale was to be repeated by his ancestors as part of their glorious pedigree.

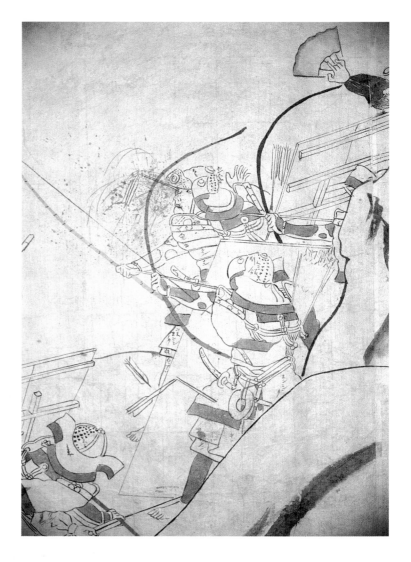

able to pull the shaft out. This infuriated Kagemasa, who could not countenance the disgrace of having someone trample on his, a samurai's, face. He leaped to his feet and attacked his friend with his sword. The arrow was eventually pulled out, but from a respectable kneeling position.

Seventy or so years later, during the Hôgen Incident of 1156, the first serious encounter in which samurai from the Taira and the Minamoto were involved, the above story was recalled by two brothers called Oba Kageyoshi and Oba Kagechika as part of their challenge to a worthy opponent:

When Hachiman-dono [Minamoto Yoshiie] attacked Kanazawa castle in Dewa in the Later Three Years' War, Kamakura Gongoro Kagemasa, at the age of sixteen, charged in the van of the battle, and while he had his left eye shot out and stuck to the first neck plate of his helmet by Toriumi Saburo, he took that enemy with his answering arrow. We are his descendants, Oba Heita Kageyoshi and his brother Saburo Kagechika.

The response to Kageyoshi's proclamation was an arrow that cut through his leg and felled his horse, and his brother had to save him from being decapitated. But the victor had indeed found a worthy opponent, just as Kajiwara Kagetoki attempted to do 28 years later at the battle of Ichi no tani. Once again the Kagemasa story was related, but note how the story has grown in the telling. Kagemasa is now credited with killing his opponent with the same arrow that wounded him:

I am Kajiwara Heizo Kagetoki, who is descended in the fifth generation from Kamakura Gongoro Kagemasa, a renowned eastern warrior who was a match for ten thousand other men. When he was sixteen he rode in the vanguard of Hachimantarô Yoshiie at the siege of Kanazawa in Dewa. He received an arrow in the left eye through his helmet, but pulled it out and with it killed the archer who loosed it, thereby acquiring honour and leaving his name for posterity.

Illustrious ancestors were precious commodities, and it is interesting to note that the same exploit was to be cited by a further descendant of Kamakura Kagemasa when he went into action during the Nanbokuchô Wars. This was 300 years after the original incident, and as the exploits of the Oba brothers and Kajiwara Kagetoki were now part of the same illustrious lineage and could now be added to the pedigree, a 14th-century samurai certainly had a lot to shout about.

THE WRITTEN PEDIGREE
It may be because of the sheer length of a pedigree by the 14th century that we come across an unusual alternative to lineage

In this print we see the use of the larger-sized flags called *nobori* in a samurai army. *Nobori* provided unit identification as distinct from personal identification. The samurai are lined up ready for battle in the formation known as *gyorin*.

proclamation. Asuke Jiro, who was active early in the Nanbokuchô Wars, provides one of the best examples of having his personal exploits written on a banner. The full inscription translates as follows:

I was born into a warrior family, and loved courage as the youth of ancient times. My military strength and determination were such that I could cut a fierce tiger to pieces. I studied the way of the bow, and learned well the techniques of warfare. Being graciously subject to the lord of heaven [i.e. the emperor], when face to face on the battlefield my desire was for a decisive encounter. At the age of 31 while having an attack of fever I went to Oyama and ran an important enemy through, holding my loyal exploits in high regard, and not partaking in immorality. My name will be praised throughout the whole world and bequeathed to my descendants as a glorious flower. Enemies strip off their armour and surrender as my vassals, I who have mastered the sword. To the righteous Hachiman Dai Bosatsu. Sincerely, Asuke Jiro of Mikawa province.

As may be expected, a samurai's family pedigree would also be written down on materials safer than war banners. Such a document would be cherished, but there can be few better examples of devotion to a written family tree than that recounted in Yamamoto Tsunetomo's *Hagakure* about the pedigree of the Soma family. The Soma mansion went up in flames, and one of the family retainers volunteered to plunge into the burning building to rescue the *daimyo's* genealogy:

he said, 'I have never been of use to my master because I am so careless, but I have lived resolved that some day my life should be of use to him. This seems to be that time.' So he leapt into the flames. After the fire had been extinguished the master said, 'Look for his remains. What a pity!' Looking everywhere they found his burnt corpse in the garden adjacent to the living quarters. When they turned it over, blood flowed out of the stomach. The man had cut open his stomach and placed the genealogy inside.

PEDIGREE AND ANONYMITY

Two developments in samurai history helped to curtail the tradition of the announcement of ancestral and personal exploits. The first was of a temporary nature, and concerned the difficulties experienced during the Mongol invasions of 1274 and 1281 when one's worthy opponent did not understand Japanese. The second developed over the centuries that followed when the use of spears and missile weapons on a large scale by lower-class *ashigaru* meant that the samurai had to hold back from going into battle until the fighting was already established. It was almost impossible to seek out a worthy opponent when one was being attacked from all sides. It was, however, at this stage in samurai history that the demands of good army organisation came most admirably to the aid of the individual warrior who wished to add another couple of paragraphs to the glorious litany of his family's military accomplishments.

Up to that time Japanese heraldry had been a comparatively rudimentary affair. Families, and often entire armies, fought under almost identical coloured flags that sometimes bore upon them the *mon* (badge) of the clan. So at the battle of Dan no Ura, for example, the defeated Taira were recognised by their red flags, and the victorious Minamoto by their white flags. During the 16th century we begin to see the use on the battlefield of the *sashimono*, a small flag flown from the back of a samurai's suit of armour. Three-dimensional objects such as fans or lacquered wooden 'sunbursts' were sometimes used instead of flags. For a prominent samurai the wearing of a *sashimono* replaced the need to proclaim one's identity in the heat of a battle. In some cases the samurai's personal *mon* would be stencilled on the *sashimono*. Other examples show the samurai's name, and for even a low-ranking retainer the appearance of his *daimyo*'s *mon* on the man's *sashimono* at least showed which side he was on. He could then seek out a worthy opponent of his own and begin a whole new chapter in his samurai lineage.

It is also apparent from the painted screens that are a major source for the appearance of 16th-century samurai armies that, in the quest for individual recognition, the *sashimono* was not enough. Wishing to make themselves noticeable above the

During the 16th century we begin to see the use on the battlefield of the *sashimono*, a small flag flown from the back of a samurai's suit of armour. Three-dimensional objects such as fans or lacquered wooden 'sunbursts' were sometimes used instead of flags. Sakai Tadatsugu is seen here with a death's head *sashimono* at the battle of Nagashino in 1575.

This woodblock print shows the second battle of Uji in 1184, when two samurai vied with each other to become the first to cross the river and enter the battle. The inclusion of *sashimono* is incorrect for the period, but illustrates how the use of such devices provided easy identification for a warrior in the heat of battle.

common herd, senior samurai frequently enhanced plain body armour by embellishing their helmets with many weird and wonderful designs of buffalo horns, peacock feather plumes, theatrical masks and conch shells. When Admiral Yi of the Korean navy won a battle against the Japanese in 1592 a collection of extraordinary helmets was among the booty taken, and Yi described them in tones of wonder in his report to the king of Korea. Huge wooden horns were a popular embellishment. Stretched versions of courtiers' caps or catfish tails were also built up using *papier maché* over an iron core. Kâto Kiyomasa owned two varieties. One was silver with a rising sun on each side, and the other was black with Kâto's 'snake's eye' *mon* in gold. Maeda Toshiie had a long golden helmet, and his son wore a similar silver one.

An alternative way in which an individual samurai might draw attention to himself was by wearing a particularly splendid helmet. Here we see Maeda Toshiie's gold catfish-tail helmet depicted on the statue of Toshiie that stands outside Kanazawa castle.

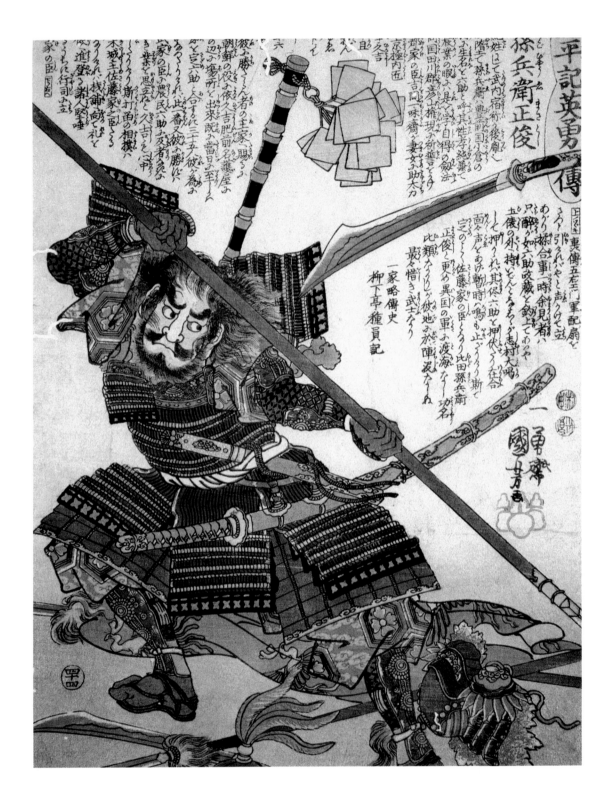

For a prominent samurai the wearing of a *sashimono* replaced the need to proclaim one's identity in the heat of a battle. Here we see the samurai Keyamura Rokusuke in action during the invasion of Korea in 1592. His *sashimono* is a three-dimensional *gohei*, a Shintô device.

THE RED BADGE OF COURAGE

Of all the ways in which one might enhance one's appearance on the battlefield, the prize must surely go to the Ii family of Hikone in Omi province (now Shiga prefecture), who dressed all their troops, both samurai and *ashigaru*, in brilliant red. The deep red that can be produced by lustrous coats of Japanese lacquer became their own unique 'red badge of courage' in the already colourful world of samurai heraldry. We will conclude this chapter with a look at the Ii family, whose pride in lineage reflects both themes dealt with above: the continuity of the samurai tradition, and its expression on the battlefield.

The name of Ii dates back to the tenth century when a member of the Fujiwara family who lived in what is now Shizuoka prefecture took the name from the village of Iinoya where his branch of the family lived. Very little is known about the early Ii until the mid-16th century, when the dominant family in the area were the Imagawa and the Ii were their vassals. The renowned general and patron of the arts Imagawa Yoshimoto (1519–60) ruled the provinces of Mikawa, Tôtômi and Suruga on the Pacific coast. Yoshimoto was a very proud and ambitious man. The location of his territories along the line of the Tokaido, the Eastern Sea Road, gave him a considerable advantage over his rivals when it came to communications, so he regarded himself as the one *daimyo* who could unite Japan once again. So in 1560 he prepared to advance on Kyôto to make the Ashikaga shogun bend to his will.

Marching with Imagawa Yoshimoto on that fateful campaign was the current head of the Ii family: Ii Naohira. Their first objective was the province of Owari, which was ruled by a minor *daimyo* called Oda Nobunaga, whose army the Imagawa outnumbered by 12 to one. At first all went well, and the Oda border fortresses began to fall to the Imagawa attacks. But Yoshimoto grew complacent, and took a break to perform the traditional head-viewing ceremony in a small wooded ravine called Okehazama. Young Oda Nobunaga seized his chance and attacked the Imagawa encampment under the cover of a fortuitous thunderstorm. Before Yoshimoto knew what was happening his head had been lopped from off his shoulders, and among the other corpses lay Ii Naohira.

The battle of Okehazama put paid to all the Imagawa ambitions. Yoshimoto was succeeded by his son Imagawa Ujizane, who tried desperately to retain the clan's lands as former allies began to desert them. When rumours grew within the Imagawa household that their vassals, the Ii, were planning to abandon, them a purge of the Ii followed. Ii Naomitsu and Ii Naoyoshi, the sons of the late Naohira, were assassinated while on their way to explain themselves to Imagawa Ujizane. Naohira's grandsons Naomori and Naochika were also murdered. The sole survivor was Naochika's three-year-old son, Naomasa, who had been born in 1561. Somehow he survived under the care of his aunt, and lived for the next few years in the protection of the temple where she was a Buddhist nun.

By the early 1570s the Imagawa had finally lost all their lands after repeated attacks from their neighbours. It seemed to be reasonably safe for Ii Naomasa to emerge from his hiding place and seek his fortune, even if he was in no position to reclaim the one that had been taken away from him. It was nonetheless important for him to ally himself with a successful local *daimyo* if he was to have any chance of success, and one local 'strong man' fortunately presented himself in the shape of Tokugawa Ieyasu of Mikawa. He had himself once been a hostage of the Imagawa and was now allied to the all-conquering Oda Nobunaga. From this moment on, the fortunes of the Ii began to flower. In 1576 Naomasa is credited with saving Ieyasu from an assassination attempt, and in 1581 he helped capture the castle of Takatenjin by draining off the water supply. In 1582 Ii Naomasa helped in the destruction of Takeda Katsuyori at the battle of Toriibata.

THE RED DEVILS

Along with grants of rice lands Ii Naomasa also received the service of many of the Takeda's old retainers, who were absorbed into the Tokugawa army after the defeat. Among these samurai were the troops who had fought for Yamagata Masakage, the renowned veteran Takeda general who had been killed at Nagashino. He was the younger brother of Obu Toramasa, who had dressed all his samurai in red armour. Tokugawa Ieyasu suggested that Ii Naomasa should copy the practice, so the Ii Red Devils were born.

In place of the usual black or brown lacquer for armour plates Ii Naomasa made a glowing red the hallmark of his retainers. The colour appeared on their body armour, their helmets, their *sashimono*, their *nobori*, their horses' harnesses and even on the minor parts of samurai armour such as the sleeves, so the Ii samurai are always the easiest to recognise on painted screens. One such screen illustrates Ii Naomasa's involvement at the battle of Nagakute in 1584. A group of *ashigaru* are firing arquebuses, while behind them we can see the great red clan banner bearing in gold the 'i' ideograph that was the first character of the family name.

Nagakute, although very bloody in its execution, was far from being an influential battle, and Toyotomi Hideyoshi and Tokugawa Ieyasu soon realised that they had little to gain from fighting each other. There followed a ritual exchange of hostages to cement the agreement. Ii Naomasa played his part by becoming the host for Hideyoshi's mother, who was held in genteel captivity in Okazaki castle for a time. By 1585 Ii Naomasa had achieved the distinction of being named as one of Tokugawa Ieyasu's four shitenno, the 'heavenly kings' who were the pillars of the Tokugawa house. In 1590 he had a further opportunity to display his skills when the Tokugawa went to war on behalf of Toyotomi Hideyoshi against the mighty Hôjô. The siege of the Hojo's Odawara castle consisted of a long blockade, and the Ii took part in one of the few pieces of real action when a mine brought down a section of Odawara's walls, and the Ii Red Devils fought their way across the breach against the Hojo samurai. This was a fierce skirmish, but ultimately the great fortress of Odawara only yielded to the spectre of starvation.

Following the successful outcome of the siege of Odawara Tokugawa Ieyasu was granted the Hojo territories in fief, and he saw to it that the loyal and reliable Ii Naomasa was suitably rewarded. Like the Tokugawa, the Ii missed the blood bath of the Korean War, and it was to be the year 1600 before they saw

In this section of the painted
screen of the Ii at Osaka in
Hikone Castle museum we see
the Red Devils of the Ii family
charging home against the samurai
of Kimura Shigenari. We are also
shown evidence of how a
sashimono could be an
encumbrance to a samurai in
combat. One samurai is fighting
his opponent with a spear while
an *ashigaru* attendant holds his
sashimono which he has withdrawn
from its carrying bucket.

action again, this time in one of the most decisive campaigns in Japanese history: Sekigahara. Ii Naomasa took a lively part in the capture of Gifu castle. He was then to be found in the Tokugawa vanguard on the fateful dark and foggy October morning, when his red-lacquered army must have been one of the few colourful sights around. Ii Naomasa had also been given personal responsibility for the safety of Matsudaira Tadayoshi, Ieyasu's fourth son, during the battle, and it is probably for this reason that the Red Devils were not actually in the front line of the vanguard, a position which they were forced to yield to Fukushima Masanori.

When the fighting commenced Ii Naomasa led his Red Devils first against the troops of Ukita Hideie, and then switched his attack to the Shimazu of Satsuma. The outcome of the battle was very much in the balance until Kobayakawa Hideaki dramatically changed sides in favour of the Tokugawa. The Shimazu pulled

Ii Naomasa made a glowing red the hallmark of his retainers. The colour appeared on their body armour, their helmets, their *sashimono*, their *nobori*, their horses' harnesses and even on the minor parts of samurai armour such as the sleeves, so the Ii samurai are always the easiest to recognise on painted screens. This screen illustrates Ii Naomasa's involvement at the battle of Sekigahara in 1600, and is in the Watanabe Museum, Tottori.

back, and as the Western Army (as the allies who opposed the Tokugawa were known) began to withdraw, the Shimazu began a gallant rearguard action, and the pursuing Ii bore the main brunt of their brave and stubborn endeavours. As the Ii pressed on there was a very dramatic development. To cover their fighting retreat, the Shimazu had stationed some arquebusiers in isolated groups as 'forlorn hope' units to ambush pursuing samurai. One of these marksmen put a well-aimed bullet into the left elbow of Ii Naomasa, and, with the pursuing commander temporarily incapacitated, the Shimazu made good their escape. We are told that his wound was dressed by Tokugawa Ieyasu himself, who blamed the wound on the heavy armour that Ii Naomasa was wearing, which seems a little unfair as the sniper hit him on one of the most exposed parts of any suit of Japanese armour.

In spite of his wound Ii Naomasa was sent to capture Sawayama castle in Omi province, the seat of the defeated Western Army leader, Ishida Mitsunari. As a reward for such loyal service Ieyasu then granted Ishida's former fief to Ii Naomasa, but as Sawayama castle had been totally destroyed during the siege, he chose to make his base a few miles away at the better location of Hikone. Over the next few years Hikone castle was built and became the family home of the Ii Red Devils. A local tradition tells us that the beautiful keep of Hikone was originally the keep of Otsu castle, which was dismantled and moved to the Hikone site. Hikone is now one of the best preserved of all Japanese castles.

The years that saw the building of Hikone witnessed such dissension within the house of Ii that it is a wonder that the family survived at all. Naomasa had two sons, the legitimate Ii Naokatsu, and Ii Naotaka, who was born to Naomasa's concubine. Naotaka's talents were so superior to those of Naokatsu that the dying Naomasa tried to ensure that Naotaka would become his heir, but when Ii Naomasa died in 1602 the agreement was torn up and the incompetent Naokatsu took over. It was fortunate for everyone that there were no current wars to fight, and Naokatsu's duties were largely confined to the construction of Hikone castle. Ii Naotaka cleverly avoided any confrontation, and continued to make himself invaluable in the eyes of Ieyasu and his son

Hidetada, who succeeded him when he retired from the post of shogun. When war came again in 1614, it was Naotaka that the Tokugawa wanted to see at the head of their irreplaceable Red Devils, not Naokatsu, so when the siege of Osaka began Ii Naotaka succeeded to the family headship, just as his father had always wanted.

One of the first actions the Red Devils were involved in at Osaka took place during the Winter Campaign of 1614–15. They attacked the huge complex of earthworks built to the south of the castle and known, from the name of its commander, as the Sanada-maru, or Sanada Barbican. The Ii were badly mauled during the fighting but would not withdraw. It is by no means clear whether this was from sheer samurai stubbornness and determination to complete the job or a simple lack of communication from headquarters in all the noise and the smoke. But those to their rear knew that the Ii had to pull back or they would be annihilated. A commander called Miura solved the problem very neatly by ordering his men to fire against the backs of the Red Devils. This had the result of forcing the Ii to 'attack to safety' when they reacted as expected, and the Red Devils survived to fight another day.

That day was not long in coming, and the Summer Campaign of Osaka in 1615 was to be the last time that the Red Devils went into battle. Their most celebrated episode, and the one shown on the screen mentioned above, was the battle of Wakae. This was one of a number of engagements that took place some distance from Osaka castle itself prior to the main assault on the fortress. The villages of Wakae and Yao, which are now suburbs of Osaka, were then tiny hamlets in the middle of rice fields. Yao was the first encounter where the Todo family on the Tokugawa side came off very badly, but out on their left flank the Red Devils soon came to grips with one of the most senior commanders on the Osaka side – Kimura Shigenari. Beginning with a volley from their arquebusiers, the Ii under Naotaka charged forward. The Kimura samurai were soon in full retreat. Kimura Shigenari was killed and his head cut off, and several of the Ii samurai claimed the credit for such an illustrious prize. When the head was taken to Tokugawa Ieyasu he noted that

TOP RIGHT The splendid collection of armour associated with the Ii family at the Watanabe Museum in Tottori. The powerful effect of the red lacquer is very apparent.

BOTTOM RIGHT This red Ii helmet is ornamented with gold *kuwagata* (horns) and is on show in the Watanabe Museum in Tottori.

A red-lacquered helmet and facemask of the Ii family in the Watanabe Museum, Tottori.

Kimura Shigenari had burned incense inside his helmet prior to the battle so as to make his severed head a more attractive trophy. Ieyasu commended the practice to his followers.

The siege of Osaka finished with the huge battle of Tennoji, which was fought on the fields to the south of the fortress, and Ii Naotaka played a major role in this, fighting alongside the survivors of the Todo against the survivors of the Kimura. A worrying moment came when a delayed-action landmine, a clever Chinese device, exploded under the Todo troops. When the army rallied and Osaka castle looked about to fall, Tokugawa Ieyasu entrusted Ii Naotaka with the task of keeping watch over Toyotomi Hideyori and his family and of securing the castle itself. Ii Naotaka interpreted these orders somewhat loosely as an invitation to open up on the castle with every piece of artillery he possessed, and soon the keep was in flames. With the fall of Osaka castle and the death of Toyotomi Hideyori all serious opposition to the Tokugawa takeover faded away, and Ii Naotaka could join his fellow *daimyo* for what would become two centuries of peace.

THE LOYAL TRADITION

The time of calm lasted until Japan was once again plunged into war with the opening up of the country to the West during the 19th century. All through this time the Ii family remained loyal supporters of the Tokugawa shoguns, and in 1860 the current head of the family, Ii Naosuke, paid for that loyalty with his life. The death of Ii Naosuke was not accomplished on a battlefield. Although one of the most senior members of the samurai class, Naosuke had probably never wielded a sword in anger in his life. His death came about as a result of his political activity on behalf of the Tokugawa shogun, to whom he was unwaveringly loyal. Ii Naosuke had been closely involved in the negotiations between the shogunate and the diplomats of countries such as the United States who sought to establish trading links with Japan from 1854 onwards. In this the shogunate had proved to be considerably far-sighted, but this was not to the liking of their rivals, who wanted to expel all the 'barbarians', as they called the Western interlopers. Ii Naosuke persisted in his belief that Japan should open its doors to the outside world, but the opposition contained many fanatics who were not averse to using their swords for political ends. One snowy winter's morning Ii Naosuke was torn from his palanquin in Edo (Tokyo) and was hacked to death by a group of anti-shogun and anti-Western terrorists who wanted to abolish the shogunate.

Ii Naosuke died a martyr for the doomed shogunate, just as his illustrious ancestor Ii Naotaka had been prepared to do at

Osaka, and his death represented one more aspect of the continuity of tradition that bound a samurai to his ancestors. Ii Naosuke had no brilliant red-lacquered armour to protect him, because traditional Japanese armour and weapons were long out of date. Any Ii men who fought for the shogun during the subsequent Restoration Wars would have been dressed in European-style military uniforms, but back in their ancestral seat of Hikone castle there still lay piles of brilliant red suits of armour. They are still there to preserve the memory of Ii Naomasa, Naotaka and Naosuke. They remind us of the Ii family's outstanding contribution to the great tradition of pride in one's samurai lineage, and their uniquely colourful means of expressing it.

CHAPTER FOUR

The samurai way of death

The death of Yamamoto Kansuke at the fourth battle of Kawanakajima in 1561 is one of the best-known instances where suicide was used to wipe away disgrace. This print by Kuniyoshi captures the agony in his face as he prepares to make amends for the failure he believed he had brought upon the Takeda family.

Although every aspect of a samurai's life is important in understanding the totality of the world of the warrior, nothing is more fundamental than a knowledge of the beliefs and traditions that surround the moment the warrior takes leave of the physical world. Whether that passing is voluntary or involuntary, the intense focus on the end of a samurai's life in so much of the relevant literature makes one very inclined to agree with the 17th-century samurai Yamamoto Tsunetomo, who wrote in his book *Hagakure* that 'the way of the samurai is found in death'.

Hagakure is a collection of short anecdotes and maxims from the traditions of the Nabeshima family, in whose samurai ranks Yamamoto Tsunetomo served. It was compiled in 1716, a good hundred years after the Period of Warring States had officially finished, but its tone is nonetheless warlike. *Hagakure* covers a vast spectrum of samurai behaviour, from the useful 'if you attach a number of bags of cloves to your body you will not be affected by inclemency and colds' to advice on bringing up children ('one should encourage bravery and avoid trivially frightening or teasing ...'). It is also delightfully snobbish in its rejection of alternative beliefs and practices in other less-favoured provinces:

The saying, 'the arts aid the body', is for samurai of other regions. For the samurai of the Nabeshima clan the arts bring ruin to the body. In all cases the person who practises an art is an artist, not a samurai ...

Yet it is the handful of passages referring directly to death that have given *Hagakure* its chilling reputation. In addition to the famous quotation with which we began this chapter, there is a long passage almost at the end of the work that reads:

Meditation on inevitable death should be performed daily. Every day when one's body and mind are at peace, one should meditate upon being ripped apart by arrows, muskets, spears and swords, being carried away by surging waves, being thrown into the midst of a great fire, being struck by lightning, being shaken to death by a great earthquake, falling from thousand-foot cliffs, dying of disease or committing seppuku at the death of one's master. And every day without fail one should consider himself as dead.

Leaving aside the references to natural disasters (and earthquakes have always been a common preoccupation in Japan), because a samurai's function in life was to fight, a calm acceptance of being 'ripped apart' might almost be regarded as the warrior's stock in trade. Nor does it set the samurai apart from any other contemporary professional fighter. The phrase that makes the samurai unique is the one about committing *seppuku* at the death of one's master. In a handful of words we are told all we need to know about the ultimate demands that might be made on the life of the samurai. The first, *seppuku*, refers to the deed itself. The second 'at the death of one's master', refers to a particular (and very controversial) set of circumstances in which the samurai might be required perform it.

SUICIDE AND THE SAMURAI

Seppuku is the correct expression for an act of suicide performed by the process of cutting open the abdomen. *Seppuku* is better known in the West as *hara kiri* (belly-cutting), and is a concept so alien to the European tradition that it is one of the few words from the world of the samurai to have entered foreign languages without a need for translation. *Seppuku* was commonly performed using a dagger. It could take place with preparation and ritual in the privacy of one's home, or speedily in a quiet corner of a battlefield while one's comrades kept the enemy at bay.

In the world of the warrior, *seppuku* was a deed of bravery that was admirable in a samurai who knew he was defeated, disgraced or mortally wounded. It meant that he could end his days with his transgressions wiped away and with his reputation not merely intact but actually enhanced. The cutting of the abdomen released the samurai's spirit in the most dramatic fashion, but it was an extremely painful and unpleasant way to die, and sometimes the samurai who was performing the act asked a loyal comrade to cut off his head at the moment of agony.

The earliest reference to *seppuku* occurs in *Hôgen Monogatari*, which deals with the conflicts in which the Taira and the Minamoto were involved in 1156. The mention of the fact that a samurai called Uno Chikaharu and his followers were captured so quickly that 'they did not have time to draw their swords or cut their bellies' is so matter-of-fact that it implies that the practice was already commonplace, at least among the warriors from eastern Japan.

The first named individual to commit *seppuku* in the war chronicles was the celebrated archer Minamoto Tametomo, who committed suicide in this way as boatloads of Taira samurai approached his island of exile. The first recorded account of *seppuku* after certain defeat in a battle that was still going on is that of Minamoto Yorimasa in the battle of Uji in 1180. His suicide was undertaken with such finesse that it was to provide a model for noble and heroic *hara kiri* for centuries to come. While his sons held off the enemy, Yorimasa retired to the seclusion of the beautiful Byodo-In temple. He then wrote a poem on the back of his war fan, which read:

Like a fossil tree
From which we gather no flowers
Sad has been my life
Fated no fruit to produce.

Minamoto Yorimasa's sequence of poem and suicide was followed many times in later history. After the battle of Yamazaki in 1582 Akechi Mitsutoshi performed the unprecedented act of committing *seppuku* and writing a poem on the door with the

The first named individual samurai in the war chronicles to commit *hara kiri* was the celebrated archer Minamoto Tametomo, who committed suicide in this way as boatloads of Taira samurai approached his island of exile. Before he went to his death Tametomo is said to have sunk one boat by holing it with an arrow. Tametomo (1139–70) was a giant of a man, and is shown here gazing out to sea before the rising sun.

blood from his abdomen, using a brush. Minamoto Yorimasa's classic act of *seppuku* was performed without the aid of a *kaishaku*, or second, to deliver a merciful blow on to his neck at the moment of agony. This was a practice that become more frequent, and much more acceptable, as the years went by, but it was never a popular duty, as Yamamoto Tsunetomo tells us:

From ages past it has been considered ill-omened by samurai to be requested as kaishaku. The reason for this is that one gains no fame even if the job is well done. And if by chance one should blunder, it becomes a lifetime disgrace.

Yamamoto Tsunetomo even gives a helpful tip concerning the performance of this most unpleasant of duties:

In the practice of past times, there were instances when the head flew off. It was said that it was best to cut leaving a little skin remaining so that it did not fly off in the direction of the verifying officials. However, at present it is best to cut clean through.

As the description earlier in this book of the mass suicide by drowning at Dan no Ura shows, *seppuku* was not the only way of ending a samurai's life, and may have been a tradition espoused only by eastern Japan until after the time of the Gempei War. No member of the Taira family is recorded as having committed *seppuku*. In other cases of alternative suicide the choice of how to end one's life was dictated by circumstances. When Imai Kanehira committed suicide at the battle of Awazu in 1184 he was surrounded by enemies, so he killed himself quickly by jumping head first from his horse with his sword in his mouth.

SUICIDE AND MOTIVATION

There are several instances in samurai history of suicide being performed as a result of personal failure. Here the samurai would commit *sokotsu-shi*, or 'expiatory suicide', the very act itself wiping the slate clean. Some later examples are quite bizarre. Legend tells us that Togo Shigechika had failed to capture a certain castle, so had himself buried alive, fully armoured and mounted on his horse, staring in the direction of his failure. Other decisions to act in this way could be spontaneous and dramatic, like the action of the veteran warrior Yamamoto Kansuke at the fourth battle of Kawanakajima in 1561. As Takeda Shingen's chief strategist he had devised the plan by which the Takeda were to surprise the Uesugi army. When his bold plan apparently failed, Kansuke took his spear and plunged into the midst of the enemy army, committing suicide to make amends for his error. The tragedy of his death was that his conclusion about the destruction of the Takeda proved incorrect. Reinforcements arrived, the army rallied, and a defeat was turned into victory. Yet an experienced general had been lost, one who would have served Shingen better by staying alive.

Committing suicide was not always a voluntary activity. It could be allowed as an honourable alternative to execution for a condemned criminal of the samurai class. Sasa Narimasa was 'invited' to commit suicide by Hideyoshi following his disastrous handling of the territory Hideyoshi had given him. *Hagakure* adds a rather extreme example:

At the fall of the castle of Arima, on the twenty-eighth day in the vicinity of the inmost citadel, Mitsue Genbei sat down on a levee between the fields. When Nakano Shigetoshi passed by and asked the reason for this, Mitsuse replied, 'I have abdominal pains and can't go a step further. I have sent the members of my group ahead, so please take command.' The situation was reported by the overseer, pronounced to be a case of cowardice, and Mitsuse was ordered to commit seppuku.

Sometimes a *daimyo* was called upon to perform *seppuku* as the basis of a peace agreement. This would so weaken the defeated clan that resistance would effectively cease. Toyotomi Hideyoshi used an enemy's suicide in this way on several occasions, of which the most dramatic, in that it effectively ended a dynasty of *daimyo* for ever, is what happened when the Hôjô were defeated at Odawara in 1590. Hideyoshi insisted on the suicide of the retired *daimyo* Hôjô Ujimasa, and the exile of his son Ujinao. With one sweep of a sword the most powerful *daimyo* family in eastern Japan disappeared from history.

Instead of the *daimyo*'s death, the victor might be satisfied with the death of his enemy's retainer if the subordinate was in charge of the castle the victor was besieging. The most theatrical example of this occurred when Hideyoshi besieged Takamatsu castle in 1582. It was a long siege, and only looked like being successful when Hideyoshi diverted a river to make a lake that gradually began to flood the castle. Hideyoshi drew up peace terms with Môri Terumoto that included the clause that the valiant defender of Takamatsu, Shimizu Muneharu, should commit suicide. Shimizu Muneharu was determined to go to his death as dramatically as he had lived, and took a boat out into the middle of the artificial lake. When he was satisfied that Hideyoshi's men were taking careful note of what he was doing he committed *seppuku*. In 1581 Tottori castle in Inaba province held out for an incredible 200 days before it surrendered to Hideyoshi. Its commander, Kikkawa Tsuneie, inspired his men

In 1581 Tottori castle in Inaba province held out for an incredible 200 days before it surrendered to Hideyoshi. Its commander, Kikkawa Tsuneie, inspired his men to this long resistance even though they were reduced to eating grass and dead horses, and may even have practised cannibalism. Tsuneie's suicide was one of the conditions of surrender, and his statue now stands in the castle grounds.

to this long resistance even though they were reduced to eating grass and dead horses, and may even have practised cannibalism. Tsuneie's suicide was one of the conditions of surrender. His letter to his son survives to this day. It reads:

We have endured for over two hundred days. We now have no provisions left. It is my belief that by giving up my life I will help my garrison. There is nothing greater than the honour of our family. I wish our soldiers to hear of the circumstances of my death.

Another reason for committing suicide was the making of a protest. This is known as *kanshi*. Examples of this are rare, but it profoundly affected one of the greatest *daimyo* of the Sengoku Period. Oda Nobunaga inherited his father's domains at the age of 15, and although he was a brave warrior he showed little interest in the administration of his territory. One of his best retainers, Hirade Kiyohide, tried in vain to persuade him to mend his ways, but when the young Nobunaga showed no inclination to listen to him Kiyohide put all his feelings into a letter to his lord, and committed *seppuku* in protest. Nobunaga was greatly moved, and changed his ways for the better, with, of course, considerable consequences for the history of Japan.

FOLLOWING IN DEATH

Junshi (following in death) is the second element in Yamamoto Tsunetomo's exhortation to preparedness for death in *Hagakure*, when he insists on a willingness to perform *seppuku* on the death of one's master. Again there are early examples to be found in the war chronicles. In *Hôgen Monogatari*, when Minamoto Yoshitomo ordered the execution of his younger brothers, the boys' attendants killed themselves immediately afterwards. Four committed *seppuku*. Two others stabbed each other. *Hôgen Monogatari* comments:

Though it was their duty to have the same death, though to go forth to the place of battle to be struck down with one's lord and to cut one's belly is the usual custom, on the grounds that there had not yet been such an example as this, there was no one who did not praise it.

When Kamakura was captured in 1333, an operation that will be described in detail later in this chapter, we read of many acts of suicide, including this classic account of *junshi*:

The retainers who were left behind ran out to the middle gate, crying aloud, 'Our lord has killed himself. Let all loyal men accompany him!' Then these twenty lit a fire in the mansion, quickly lined up together in the smoke and cut their bellies. And not willing to be outdone, three hundred other warriors cut their bellies and leapt into the consuming flames.

There are examples of *junshi* being performed even before the *daimyo* was dead. Shortly before Shimizu Muneharu's dramatic suicide on the artificial lake of Takamatsu in 1582, one of his

A good example of a willingness to follow one's lord in death is provided by Kojima Shingoro, who came to Kitanosho castle to serve his master Shibata Katsuie at the time of the Shizugatake campaign in 1583. In spite of illness, Shingoro joined the garrison and wrote a pledge on the castle gate.

This print by Kuniyoshi shows the delicate balance in samurai culture between the aesthetic and the warlike principles. Matsunaga Hisahide (1510–77) has been defeated by Oda Nobunaga at his castle of Shikizan, and before he prepares to commit *hara kiri* he smashes the priceless tea kettle called 'Hiragumo' so that it will not fall into the hands of his enemies.

retainers invited Muneharu to his room. The loyal retainer explained that he wished to reassure his master about the ease with which *seppuku* could be performed. He explained that he had in fact already committed suicide, and, pulling aside his robe, showed Muneharu his severed abdomen. Muneharu was touched by the gesture, and acted as his retainer's second to bring the act to a speedy and less painful conclusion by cutting off the man's head.

Although *Hôgen Monogatari* commends the practice, *junshi* was the one reason for committing suicide that did not meet with universal approval. However inspiring the example may have been to one's fellow samurai, there were many circumstances when *junshi* merely added more unnecessary deaths to an existing disaster. The death of a *daimyo* may or may not have brought about the extinction of his house, but the practice of *junshi* by the senior retainers who would otherwise support and guide the lord's infant heir only made extinction more likely. A spontaneous gesture on the battlefield was understandable and even forgivable, and in the confusion of a battle the circumstances of a retainer's death could never be clearly established. But when the death of a *daimyo* from natural causes during times of peace provoked the performance of *junshi* such an act was almost universally condemned. In such cases a loyal retainer committed suicide to show that he could serve none other than his departed lord. During the Sengoku Period some retainers did have little left to live for, but in the later times of peace *junshi* was hardly helpful in maintaining the stability of a dynasty. In the early Edo Period as many as 20 leading retainers of various *daimyo* were known to have committed *junshi* on the deaths of their lords.

A better way to serve one's departed lord, the shogun argued, was to render equally loyal service to his heir, but *junshi* was firmly engrained in the Japanese mentality. A strong condemnation of it is found in the so-called Legacy of Ieyasu, the House Laws left by the first Tokugawa shogun in 1616. But at the death of his grandson the third Tokugawa shogun, Iemitsu, in 1651, five of the leading retainers of the Tokugawa committed *junshi*, a remarkable gesture against the law they themselves had formulated. A further attempt to ban it was introduced by the shogunate in 1663, and included the statement:

In the event that a lord has a presentiment that a certain vassal is liable to immolate himself, he should admonish him strongly against it during his lifetime. If he fails to do so, it shall be counted as his fault. His heir will not escape appropriate punishment.

Five years later an instance of *junshi* occurred among the retainers of the recently deceased *daimyo* of the house of Okudaira, but little action was taken against the family because of the great service the Okudaira had rendered to the Tokugawa in previous years. Their ancestor had been the defender of Nagashino castle at the time of the famous battle. The family of the actual performer of *junshi* were not so fortunate. His two sons were ordered to commit *seppuku*, and his two sons-in-law, one of whom was of the Okudaira family, were exiled. Other *daimyo*s finally took note, and from the mid-17th century onwards the practice of *junshi* effectively ceased until it came dramatically to the attention of modern Japan in 1912. On the eve of the funeral of Emperor Meiji, General Nogi and his wife committed suicide. Nogi had commanded troops in the Sino-Japanese War of 1894–95, and led the battle to take Port Arthur in the Russo-Japanese War of 1904–05. It was an act that astounded his contemporaries because of the bizarre disloyalty to the emperor's wishes that the illegal act implied. It was also sobering evidence that the samurai spirit lived on in the Japan of the 20th century.

SUICIDE AS A GROUP ACTIVITY

Reference was made earlier to the tension between the needs of the samurai as an individual warrior and the needs of the group to which he belonged, a definition that almost always meant the army of the *daimyo* whom he was sworn to serve. The tradition of ritual suicide was the most dramatic individual gesture that any samurai could make, but occasionally in samurai history we see the act of suicide as a group expression. The battle of Dan no Ura has already been presented as an important example, but in this chapter we will move forward two centuries to the epic of the 14th-century Nanbokuchô Wars called the *Taiheiki*. Here we see a remarkable interplay between the samurai as an individual and the samurai as a member of a group. In the story of how Nitta Yoshisada (1301–38) captured Kamakura in 1333, we see these tensions at their most revealing. His victory caused a mass act of suicide, while his own death just five years later represents the other extreme. We now see a lonely, failed warrior, whose death retains his honour and adds another chapter to the story of samurai greatness as part of the tremendous continuity to be found within the world of the samurai.

The fall of Kamakura

Kamakura, which is nowadays a pleasant seaside town, was the capital for the Minamoto *bakufu* and the Hôjô *shikken*. Kyôto was relegated to the status of the divine emperor's home, and

The most famous legend of the siege of Kamakura in 1333 concerns Nitta Yoshisada and his offering to the Sun Goddess of his sword. The *Taiheiki* tells us, 'So he prayed, and cast his gold-mounted sword into the sea. May it not be that the dragon-gods accepted it? At the setting of the moon that night, suddenly for more than 2,000 yards (1,880m) the waters ebbed away from Inamura Cape, where for the first time a broad flat beach appeared.'

little else. All the important decisions were made in Kamakura, which was set in the heartlands of the fierce eastern warriors, so that the century and a half between 1192 and 1333 is known as the Kamakura Period in Japanese history.

The challenge to the rule of the Hôjô came from the attempt at imperial restoration launched by Emperor Go Daigo in 1331. We noted earlier how Go Daigo took refuge in the mountains under the protection of Kusunoki Masashige, but he also needed a warrior family in the east to take the war directly against the Hôjô. Such a man was found in the person of Nitta Yoshisada. Yoshisada had previously served the Hôjô army and had in fact pitted himself and his samurai against Kusunoki Masashige's mountain strongholds. His reasons for changing sides and joining Go Daigo were different from Kusunoki's. The Kusunoki had been tenants of imperial lands for centuries, and owed allegiance to the emperor as to an ordinary feudal lord. The Nitta were much more humble, and therefore had much more to gain by picking the winning side. They were related to the Ashikaga, but were regarded as being of inferior status because, at the time of the Gempei War, an ancestor had committed the unforgivable sin of failing to respond to Yoritomo's call to arms. As a result, he had not benefited from Yoritomo's generosity in the same way as other families had, such as the Hôjô. There were therefore sound reasons for the Nitta to be envious of the Hôjô, so they now threw in their lot with Go Daigo, hoping that this time they were supporting an eventual victor.

Nitta's defection to the imperial cause came in 1333, shortly after he had received orders from the Hôjô to continue the siege of Masashige's castle of Chihaya. By sending messages on ahead to samurai in his home province whom he knew would support him, Nitta Yoshisada was able to return to Kozuke in June 1333 and proclaim his rebellion. It was soon obvious that he intended to attack Kamakura directly, so Hôjô Takatoki sent a force out to meet him, which engaged Nitta as he was attempting to cross the Tamagawa river. He was not stopped, and Kamakura lay at his mercy.

As the administrative capital of Japan, Kamakura had grown rapidly during its heyday, and numerous important edifices, which today make Kamakura one of the most fascinating Japanese cities to visit, date from the Kamakura Period. The city is still squeezed in by mountains on three sides and the sea on a fourth. The topography is best appreciated nowadays from the train, which winds its way through tunnels and cuttings to reach Kamakura, and these hills were no less important in 1333 as they formed the main, natural outer defences of the Hôjô's headquarters. Seven passes guarded by checkpoints ran through these hills. The western approach to Kamakura was covered by the Daibutsu Pass, which drops down beside one of Kamakura's most famous sights, the Great Buddha. This huge and beautiful bronze statue witnessed the fighting in 1333, although none of the combatants would have seen it as one does today as, at that time, it was concealed within a wooden temple building, much like the other Great Buddha at the Todaiji in Nara. In 1335, and again in 1368, violent storms all but wrecked the building, and then in 1495 a *tsunami* (freak wave) swept away all remnants of the structure to leave the Buddha sitting in the open air.

The western approach to Kamakura was covered by the Daibutsu Pass, which drops down beside one of Kamakura's most famous sights, the Great Buddha. This huge and beautiful bronze statue witnessed the fighting in 1333, although none of the combatants would have seen it as one does today. At that time it was concealed within a wooden temple building, much like the other Great Buddha at the Todaiji in Nara. In 1335, and again in 1368, violent storms all but wrecked the building, and then in 1495 a *tsunami* swept away all remnants of the structure to leave the Buddha sitting in the open air.

Nitta Yoshisada leads the attack on Kamakura along the beach. This was followed by heavy fighting within the city. Mass graves have been discovered where the fighting took place in 1333.

Nitta Yoshisada divided his forces into three divisions to attack from the north, east and west. The *Taiheiki* describes the fighting in great detail, using such hyperbolic expressions as:

When a son was stricken, his father did not minister to him, but rode over his body to attack the enemy in front; when a lord was shot down from his horse by an arrow, his retainer did not raise him up, but mounted on to the horse and galloped forward.

In spite of hours of fierce fighting, no real breakthrough had been achieved by the loyalists, particularly on the western side where the Gokurakuji Pass was held firmly behind rows of stout wooden shields. Nitta Yoshisada went there himself to take a closer look, and realised that there was a chance of bypassing Gokurakuji altogether if it were possible to round the cape where the promontory of Inamuragasaki projects into the sea. There was a small expanse of beach at low tide, but the tide was then high, and the Hôjô had taken the added precaution of placing several ships at a short distance from the shore, from which a barrage of arrows could cover any flanking attack. At this point there occurred the event that gave rise to the great legend of the battle of Kamakura, because Nitta Yoshisada threw his sword into the sea as an offering to the Sun Goddess, and the waters parted to let his army through. Once Nitta Yoshisada's troops were in the city the battle became a fierce hand-to-hand struggle among the burning houses, while the Hôjô forces were torn between holding the passes and resisting the new advance round the cape. The *Taiheiki* is driven to use Hindu and Buddhist cosmology to convey to its readers the horror of the fighting as the loyalists swept into the city:

Fires were lighted among the commoners' houses along the beach, and also east and west of the Inase river, where from flames like carriage wheels flew and scattered in black smoke ... Entering clamorously beneath the fierce flames, the warriors of the Genji [the imperialists] everywhere shot the bewildered enemy with arrows, cut them down with their swords, grappled with them, and stabbed them ... Surely even thus was the battle of Indra's palace, when the asuras fell onto the swords and halberds, punished by the ruler of heaven! Even thus is the plight of sinners in the Hell of Constant Scorching, who sink to the bottom of the molten iron, driven by jailers' whips!

Immolation at Kamakura

When the battle was seen to be lost, the Hôjô family and their closest retainers decided to die like true samurai, and the *Taiheiki* has preserved the gory record of their departure. Once again we have the spectacle of the members of a defeated samurai army taking their own lives, but there are several interesting differences from the situation at Dan no Ura. At Dan no Ura the decision to die by drowning was made at the last minute. We therefore see no examples of rituals such as the writing of a farewell poem. At Kamakura the defeated Hôjô had more time to prepare, and the *Taiheiki* recounts the process in detail. So, for example, we read how a certain warrior monk called Fuonji Shinnin wrote a poem on a pillar inside a temple using his own blood while he committed *seppuku*. It read:

Wait awhile
Traversing together the road of Shideyama
Let us talk of the transient world.

Another monk used his trousers as a writing surface for his death poem with the words:

Holding the trenchant hair-splitter
He severs emptiness
Within the mighty flames
A pure cool breeze.

The monk then commanded his son to decapitate him. After performing the deed, the tearful son took the long sword and plunged it through his own body. At this three of their retainers ran up and impaled themselves in turn on the protruding blade, so that they fell down 'with their heads in a row like fish on a skewer' as the *Taiheiki* so eloquently puts it. Women too committed suicide as the news of the fall of Kamakura spread:

Heedless of men's eyes, the weeping nurse called Osai ran after
him barefoot for five or six hundred yards, falling down to the
ground again and again … And when her eyes beheld him no
longer, the nurse Osai cast her body into a deep well and perished.

It was only fitting that the closest members of the Hôjô family should perform the most dramatic act of suicide. They withdrew from their positions to a temple called the Tôshôji, a rather ironic name which means 'the temple of the victory in the east'. Here, they made ready to commit suicide in the privacy of a cave dug out of the rock at the rear within the temple compound. The Tôshôji no longer exists, but the so-called 'hara kiri cave' is still there, and although it lies in a remote wooded spot on the fringe of the city centre, it still attracts many pilgrims. It is rare to visit it and not see fresh flowers left as an offering.

Several of the senior family members were concerned that their leader Hôjô Takatoki would not have the courage to commit hara kiri himself, so the others decided to set a precedent. Inside the temple, one samurai 'cut his body with a long cut from left to right and fell down, pulling out his intestines ...'. Nearby another exemplary suicide took place between a grandfather and his grandson. Nagasaki Shin'uemon, a young boy 15 years old that year, bowed before his grandfather saying, 'Assuredly will the Buddhas and kami give sanction to this deed. The filial descendant is he who brings honour to the name of his father.' With two thrusts of his dagger he slashed the veins of his aged grandfather's arms. He then cut his own belly, pushing his grandfather down, and fell on top of him.

The young boy's example provided the stimulus that Hôjô Takatoki needed, and he too committed seppuku. The Taiheiki gives a number of 283 'men of the Hôjô' who took their lives in the Tôshôji. That number was to grow, because:

> a fire was lighted in the hall, where from fierce flames leapt up and black smoke darkened the sky. When the warriors in the courtyard and before the gate beheld that fire, some among them cut their bellies and ran into the flames, while others smote one another with their swords and fell down together in a heap, fathers, sons and brothers. As a great river was the rushing of their blood; as on a burial field were their dead bodies laid everywhere in heaps! Although the bodies of these disappeared in the flames, later it was known that more than eight hundred and seventy men perished in this one place.

As the news spread into Kamakura itself, many more people followed the Hôjô in death – 'more than six thousand persons'

When Kamakura fell, the Hôjô leaders withdrew from their positions to a temple called the Tôshôji, a rather ironic name that means 'the temple of the victory in the east'. Here, they made ready to commit suicide in the privacy of a cave dug out of the rock at the rear within the temple compound. The Tôshôji no longer exists, but the so-called 'hara kiri cave' is still there. Although it lies in a remote wooded spot on the fringe of the city centre, it still attracts many pilgrims.

says the *Taiheiki*. Thus passed the Hôjô regency in a massive bloodbath almost unparalleled in samurai history. They were the family who had defeated the Mongols and presided over one of the most peaceful centuries in Japanese history. But when they departed out of history they did so in an unprecedented fashion that exceeded the demands made by samurai tradition.

Evidence of how fierce the fighting at Kamakura really was has recently come to light with the excavation and analysis of grave pits in the Zaimokuza area, a district near the sea where the Hôjô made their last stand. Many skulls and fragments of weapons have been found, which have been studied by archaeologists. The pattern of wounds to the head indicate that none of the victims wore much in the way of head protection, which inclines one to the view that these grave pits were mass burial grounds for the common soldiers. The samurai were buried elsewhere, and for centuries there was a traditional belief in Kamakura that many were interred in burial caves in the hills. The local rock is quite soft, and there are 50 or so burial niches in the walls of the Shakado Tunnel, which was cut through a hill leading to the north-east of Kamakura in about 1250. In 1965 the tradition of victims of the battle being buried here was confirmed when a landslip revealed a tombstone bearing the very date, 10 July 1333, when the city fell to Nitta Yoshisada.

THE LONELY DEATH OF NITTA YOSHISADA

We conclude this chapter with one of the most interesting accounts of an individual warrior's suicide in the whole of samurai history, in which several of the elements discussed above come together. The samurai is Nitta Yoshisada, the conqueror of Kamakura. In marked contrast to the mass suicide of the Hôjô, Yoshisada's own death was a lonely one in a bleak setting in Echizen province.

Nitta Yoshisada became the samurai general on whom Emperor Go Daigo particularly depended after the death of Kusunoki Masashige at the battle of Minatogawa in 1336. By 1338 the balance of power between Ashikaga Takauji and Go Daigo's loyalists had become very uncertain, and nowhere was this more apparent than in the distant provinces of the north-east on the Sea of Japan coast. Nitta Yoshisada's final campaign saw him being despatched by Go Daigo to capture the fortress of Fujishima, an ordinary wooden stockade enclosure defended by warrior monks, whose military skills Nitta Yoshisada despised. But certain portents on his way into battle gave him cause for concern. First Yoshisada's horse reared and almost trampled to death two of his grooms. Then as the army were crossing a river Yoshisada's standard- bearer's horse collapsed and threw its rider into the water clutching the Nitta banner.

More serious was the determined resistance put up by the monks of Fujishima. Realising that he would have to take the lead if his men were to break through, Yoshisada led the way through the rice fields, where the enemy's footsoldiers had erected wooden shields and began to loose hundreds of arrows at him. Yoshisada's mounted attendants tried to form a line in front of him to protect him from the archery, but one by one they were struck down and killed. His comrades urged him to withdraw, but Yoshisada ignored them and drove his horse forward into the attack. The poor animal then received an arrow and fell like a folding screen, trapping Yoshisada's left leg under its body. At that moment an arrow smashed through Yoshisada's helmet and into his forehead. Still conscious, Yoshisada committed suicide, but not by *hara kiri*. There was no time for that, nor did his trapped position allow him to reach his abdomen. Instead Nitta Yoshisada is said to have cut off his own head. It rolled into a rice paddy and his body slid in after it. To cut off one's own head sounds far-fetched, but in the heat of the battle and with a samurai sword of legendary sharpness it is entirely believable of someone with Yoshisada's fanaticism and in such desperate straits.

Yamamoto Tsunetomo was particularly impressed with the example of Nitta Yoshisada and refers to his death twice in *Hagakure*. In one mention he refers to a strange belief concerning Yoshisada – that he carried on fighting after his head was cut off:

Even if one's head were to be suddenly cut off, he should be able to do one more action with certainty. The last moments of Nitta Yoshisada are proof of this. Had his spirit been weak, he would have fallen the moment his head was severed.

It was an example that certainly impressed Nitta Yoshisada's followers too, because several of his senior samurai immediately performed *junshi* next to his body. This shows great devotion on the part of the Nitta samurai, but their act of following in death

In marked contrast to the mass suicide of the Hôjô at Kamakura, Nitta Yoshisada's own death was a lonely one in a bleak setting in Echizen province. In this fine modern print we see how Yoshisada's horse was shot from under him, but, unlike the account in the *Taiheiki*, Yoshisada is shown rising to his feet to meet his enemies. He is also said to have cut off his own head.

stands in marked contrast to what happened next, because Yoshisada's brother Nitta Yoshisuke resolved to lead another Nitta army 'to die in the place where their general died'. But the passage of a couple of days had allowed time for reflection, and the prospect of going on a suicide mission for a cause that was already lost did not appeal to the majority of his army, who either deserted, took Buddhist vows or joined the enemy. Following in death, the most dramatic gesture that a samurai could make, was most easily accomplished when there was little time to think about it. Yamamoto Tsunetomo's exhortation in *Hagakure* from the peaceful days of 1716 did not apply completely to the bitter days of real samurai warfare.

CHAPTER FIVE

Weapons of mass destruction

The death of a samurai is shown in this very dramatic print by Kuniyoshi. He is named as Yamanaka Dankuro, and appears to have received a spear thrust into his stomach, although the clouds of smoke billowing around may intend us to understand that the spear shaft is actually the path of a bullet.

The samurai is probably the only warrior in history whose traditional weapon is as well known as the warrior himself. The Gurkhas may be renowned for their *kukris* and the Vikings for their broad axes, but there is no more celebrated union of warrior and weapon than the samurai and his sword. Forged by master craftsmen to a standard of metallurgy that contemporary Europe can only have dreamed of, the samurai sword was the deadliest of weapons, the most cherished of possessions, and, in the words of Shogun Tokugawa Ieyasu, nothing less than the 'soul of the samurai'.

It is therefore somewhat sobering to find that in the harsh reality of samurai warfare the Japanese sword was never that highly regarded. All samurai carried swords and used them to good effect, but in battle no samurai ever relied solely on his sword. Nor were all swords of the superlative quality that traditional views would have us believe. Broken blades are frequently reported, and a samurai could also be put at a disadvantage when his sword got stuck in the body of an opponent that he had just killed. One warrior is recorded uttering a prayer that his sword might be dislodged from his enemy's corpse! Almost no references in *Heike Monogatari* deal exclusively with swordplay. Instead the use of the sword is but one stage in a process that begins with the bow, moves through the sword to the dagger, and often ends with bare hands.

During the formative years of the samurai tradition the most important weapon was actually the bow. The first expression that we come across in the earliest war chronicles and epic poetry to describe the samurai's calling makes no reference to a sword. Instead the phrase used is the 'way of horse and bow'. The first samurai were mounted archers, and it was by his skill in loosing arrows from horseback that a warrior's prowess was judged. The technique was practised endlessly, and gave rise to the colourful martial art of *yabusame*, whereby mounted archers try to hit wooden targets at the gallop. *Yabusame* may still be seen in Japan today at festivals.

Historical records give us a fair idea of the efficacy of arrows fired from the Japanese longbow. A direct hit between the eyes that avoided the peak of a samurai's helmet and the facemask would of course be instantly fatal, but it was more common for samurai to die after sustaining multiple arrow hits. This was largely due to the stopping power of their armour, and the popular image from woodblock prints of the dying samurai crawling along like a porcupine with hundred of arrows protruding from him is not too much of an exaggeration. A certain Imagawa Yorikuni, who fought during the Nanbokuchô Wars, needed 20 arrows to kill him. It was only when the arrows were spent that the mounted archer became a samurai swordsman.

As time went by another consideration began to militate against the samurai being seen as an individual swordsman and nothing else. Armies were growing in size, and the *ashigaru* had to be armed with the finest weapons that a *daimyo* could afford. Large numbers inevitably ruled out top quality, leading to one *daimyo* commenting that if a thousand spears could be purchased for the price of one superlative sword then it should be the spears that made their way into the samurai shopping basket. But spears were just one weapon in the *ashigaru* armoury. The footsoldiers were also issued with bows, thus destroying for ever the image of the samurai as an elite mounted archer. Yet neither spears, swords nor bows were to be responsible for the military revolution that transformed Japanese warfare during the Period of Warring States. This was brought about by the introduction of firearms.

The first guns came to Japan from China in 1510 and consisted of a short iron tube fixed to a long wooden shaft. The barrel was wider around its touch hole and had a slightly conical muzzle terminating in an elongated aperture. Pictures of similar European models show the stock of the gun being held tightly under the left arm while the right hand applied the lighted match. This type of gun is known to have been used in battle as late as 1548 at Uedahara, but it was never widely adopted in Japanese warfare and was immediately scrapped following the dissemination of a much more sophisticated model. This was the arquebus, introduced from Portugal in 1543. Its arrival was unexpected and completely unheralded, being just one very interesting item of exotica possessed by an unfortunate band of Portuguese traders whose wrecked ship was washed up on the Japanese island of Tanegashima in 1543. Tanegashima happened to be owned by the Shimazu of Satsuma, one of the most warlike samurai families in Japan. So when the Portuguese arranged a demonstration of the new weapons the local *daimyo* saw instantly what a wonderful opportunity had come his way and his most skilled swordsmiths suddenly became gunsmiths. On the most conservative estimate ten arquebuses were manufactured in Satsuma over the following year, although Mendes Pinto, the Portuguese traveller who was much given to exaggeration, put the number at 600. Yet even Pinto was hardly exaggerating when he explained the great popularity of the new weapons as being due to the Japanese 'being naturally addicted to the wars, wherein they take more delight than any other nation we know'.

The arquebus was a simple muzzle-loading musket fired by a lighted match that was dropped on to the pan when the trigger was pulled. It was already revolutionising European warfare, and similar models had helped bring about the victory of the Spanish general Gonzalo de Cordoba at Cerignola in 1503. Gonzalo had been faced with heavily armoured French knights who were used to breaking an enemy position by a fierce frontal charge. At Cerignola, Gonzalo had the privilege of selecting his own position, so he chose to act defensively by digging a ditch, reinforcing it with stakes, and creating a front line in which as many as 2,000 arquebusiers may have been deployed in four ranks. Japan provided no parallel with Cerignola until the battle of Nagashino in 1575, where the Takeda clan took the role of the

The first samurai were mounted archers, and it was by his skill in loosing arrows from horseback that a warrior's prowess was judged. The technique was practised endlessly and gave rise to the colourful martial art of *yabusame*, whereby mounted archers dressed in hunting costume try to hit wooden targets at the gallop. *Yabusame* may still be seen in Japan today at festivals.

French at Cerignola and suffered a similar disaster when massed ranks of arquebuses broke their charge.

After Nagashino the use of large numbers of arquebuses became commonplace. As for larger-scale firearms, it is generally believed that the samurai made very little use of cannon or indeed any form of heavy artillery until the last major campaign of the Period of Warring States at Osaka between 1614 and 1615. However, the bombardments that were to prove so effective at Osaka were preceded by several little-known artillery engagements during the previous half-century. One reason why these are so obscure is because they were confined to the wars between the samurai families of the island of Kyûshû, so it is to their rivalries that we must first turn.

THE SHIMAZU OF SATSUMA

We noted above that Japan's first arquebuses made landfall in the territories owned by the Shimazu of Satsuma. The Shimazu were the great survivors in the world of the warrior. Their location in Satsuma province, the southernmost tip of the main Japanese islands, gave them an independence from central government control that the Shimazu cherished and defended for centuries. During the 16th century they expanded northwards until at their peak the Shimazu ruled most of Kyûshû. They were on the point of overcoming their great rivals, the Otomo, when nemesis appeared in the shape of Toyotomi Hideyoshi, the unifier of Japan. Two massive armies invaded Kyûshû in 1587 and drove the Shimazu back to their homeland of Satsuma. Fortunately for them, the accommodative method practised by Hideyoshi allowed them to retain their ancestral lands, so there were Shimazu *daimyo* in Satsuma up until the time of the Meiji Restoration.

The eight centuries of Shimazu rule began with the first Shimazu, Tadahisa, who was an illegitimate son of Minamoto Yoritomo. His mother was hounded out of Kamakura by Yoritomo's wife and gave birth to Tadahisa, who grew up to serve his father in war. Mindful, perhaps, of his wife's feelings on the matter, Yoritomo made Tadahisa governor of Satsuma, which was about as far from Kamakura as it was physically possible to reach. He settled in Kagoshima where the family prospered, and four centuries later his descendant Takahisa (1514–71) was ruling from Kagoshima as the 15th Shimazu *daimyo*. Their remote location so far from the centres of Japanese government kept the Shimazu at the periphery of samurai affairs for many years until 1543 when the fateful Portuguese ship was washed up on the island of Tanegashima. Satsuma changed overnight from being an obscure backwater of Japan to becoming its main gateway to the West. A few years later Shimazu Takahisa was to make history again by becoming the first *daimyo* to use firearms in warfare. That same year (1549) he also entertained St Francis Xavier on the latter's first arrival in Japan. Two important innovations: guns and Christianity, had therefore appeared on the Shimazu lands. Takahisa embraced

On his death in 1571 the *daimyo* of Satsuma Shimazu Takahisa bequeathed to posterity not one but four samurai sons whose military exploits were to dominate the affairs of southern Japan for half a century to come. The eldest was Yoshihisa (1533–1611), shown here in this print.

the first but never succumbed to the lure of the second, no matter what benefits it might bring.

On his death Shimazu Takahisa bequeathed to posterity not one but four samurai sons whose military exploits were to dominate the affairs of southern Japan for half a century to come. The eldest was Yoshihisa (1533–1611), who was served loyally by his three brothers. Yoshihiro (1535–1619) fought against the Otomo and took the main brunt of the invasion of Kyûshû by Toyotomi Hideyoshi in 1587. He also led the Satsuma contingent during the Korean War. The third son Toshihisa (1537–92) suffered poor health and died before he could see service in that ill-fated expedition, while Iehisa (1547–87) was assassinated as Hideyoshi's army swept through Kyûshû.

Having the advantage of a large and loyal army, the Shimazu were able to co-ordinate their movements in a way many other *daimyo* may have envied. Their favourite move was the use of a decoy force to draw an advance from the enemy. The decoy unit would then go into a rapid and controlled false retreat, stimulating pursuit. Other units of the Shimazu would lie to the flanks in ambush, with the main body held back. The Shimazu operated the decoy system on eight occasions between 1527 and 1600. All but one was successful, the failure being Sekigahara in 1600, where the Shimazu were but one army among others in a force doomed by the defection of an ally. Otherwise the system enabled the Shimazu to be victorious even against overwhelming odds at the battle of Kizakihara in 1573 against the Ito, and the battle of Okita-Nawate in 1584 against the Ryûzôji, where the ratio was ten to one in each case.

Shimazu Yoshihiro was probably the most colourful of the four Shimazu brothers. Yoshihiro (1535–1619) fought against the Otomo and took the main brunt of the invasion of Kyûshû by Toyotomi Hideyoshi in 1587. He also led the Satsuma contingent during the Korean War. This fine equestrian statue of him stands outside Ijuin railway station, near Kagoshima.

THE OTOMO OF BUNGO

The Otomo family were one of a handful of great *daimyo* families who shared Kyûshû with the Shimazu. They were of Fujiwara stock, but tradition accords to the first Otomo an origin not dissimilar to that of his Shimazu contemporary. Once again the illegitimate offspring fought loyally for the Minamoto and was rewarded with lands as far away from Yoritomo's wife as possible. The Otomo settled in Bungo province in north-eastern Kyûshû, and Otomo

Otomo Sôrin Yoshishige (1530–87) embraced European trade, culture, weapons and (ultimately) its religion with an enthusiasm that was unparalleled among his contemporaries. His conversion to Christianity stood in marked contrast to the Shimazu attitude and made Yoshishige the darling of the Jesuits. This statue of him stands outside Oita station.

Yoshinori was the head of the Otomo family at the time of the arrival of Europeans at Tanegashima. The news of the strange weapons they had brought with them soon reached Yoshinori's ears. Not wishing to be upstaged by the Shimazu, he invited the Portuguese visitors to his castle of Funai (modern Oita) to give a further demonstration. Yoshinori was much impressed, but his acquisition of new technology was not sufficient to prevent him from being assassinated by one of his own retainers in 1550.

Yoshinori was succeeded by his son Yoshishige (1530–87), who embraced European trade, culture, weapons and (ultimately) its religion with an enthusiasm that was unparalleled among his contemporaries. His conversion to Christianity stood in marked contrast to the Shimazu attitude and made Yoshishige the darling of the Jesuits. As his name appears so often in their reports home we know a great deal about the Otomo court. For example, an account of a banquet thrown by Otomo Yoshishige for some European visitors in 1556 contains probably the earliest European observation on the use of chopsticks: 'for all their people are accustomed to eat with two sticks, they think it very dirty to eat with the hands as we are wont to do'.

In 1562 Yoshishige left the administration of Funai castle to his son and made a new headquarters for himself in the castle of Usuki. It was at this point that he shaved his head and became a Buddhist monk under the name of Sôrin, and it is as Otomo Sôrin that this future Christian *daimyo* is best known. With his ego and his arsenal continually boosted by his European connections, Sôrin pursued an expansionist policy, gobbling up smaller fry in neighbouring provinces until the limits of Otomo territory collided with the similarly expansive borders of the mighty Shimazu of Satsuma. In 1578, the same year that Otomo Sôrin finally accepted Christian baptism, the two sides met in battle.

CANNON AND THE OTOMO

The introduction of hand-held firearms to Japan is associated particularly with the Shimazu, but to the Otomo must be credited the development of the use of cannon, a topic tabout which comparatively little is known by comparison. However, the first use of Portuguese cannon in battle by the Otomo was a very curious affair, because the cannon in question were still attached to Portuguese ships! This battle happened in 1561 and involved an attack on the Môri clan's strategic fortress of Moji, a castle that overlooked the straits of Shimonoseki between Honshu and Kyûshû. Moji had changed hands several times between 1557 and 1561. In 1561 a number of Portuguese ships were anchored at Funai. Otomo Sôrin's contacts with the friendly Europeans had boosted their trade, and they were now to use that relationship in a way never seen before in Japanese history, because Sôrin invited the Portuguese to assist him by bombarding Moji castle from the sea.

For the Portuguese to accept was a very risky step that threatened to imperil the delicate relationship they had built up with the Japanese. To be seen to be so partisan towards one friendly *daimyo* that they would assist him in war against a neighbour was an act that could threaten the existence of other traders and missionaries elsewhere in Japan. It was also very risky to be seen attacking the Môri, as their city of Yamaguchi was another well-established centre of Japanese Christianity. But the Portuguese agreed, and three ships sailed northwards into the straits of Shimonoseki and opened up against the defenders of Moji castle.

Each ship was of between 500 and 600 tons, with 300 crew and 17 or 18 cannon. With their guns at as high an elevation as was possible, Moji was bombarded. Never before had Japanese troops been subjected to the firepower of European ships, so the effects on the garrison were dramatic. The cannonballs smashed the wooden and bamboo fences and caused many casualties, but the effect on morale was the most severe. The castle would almost certainly have fallen immediately had it not been for the fact that the Portuguese ships had not come to Japan expecting to be used in warfare, but were armed merely for self-defence. As a result, Sôrin's foreign allies very soon ran out of cannonballs. Once their ammunition was exhausted they had no further role to play, so they turned and sailed back to Funai.

The Portuguese action had nonetheless served a very useful purpose in keeping the garrison occupied while the Otomo army surrounded the promontory on which Moji was built. But once the ships withdrew, the Môri commanders realised that their command of the straits had not been permanently challenged. They decided to reinforce the garrison by sea, and rowed across in the manner of a suicide squad. The Môri troops managed to land, pierced the Otomo lines and entered Moji castle to reinforce and re-inspire its garrison. When he realised that the Portuguese ships were unlikely to return, Otomo Sôrin ordered an all-out assault on Moji. The attack failed, and Moji was left as a Môri possession. This caused a long-term embarrassment to the Otomo, who soon had other problems on their hands in the shape of the Shimazu.

We do not know for certain the types of cannon carried by the Portuguese ships at Moji, but the next we hear of cannon in the possession of the Otomo the guns are clearly heavy bronze breech-loading swivel guns. The typology of 'swivel guns' arises from the fact that the trunnions rotated vertically within a swivel-yoke bracket that was itself mounted to rotate horizontally. The element of breech-loading, which we tend to think of as a modern artillery innovation, has in fact a long history in European gunnery. Instead of being rammed down from the muzzle, the ball, powder and wad were introduced into the breech inside a sturdy chamber shaped like a large tankard with a handle. A metal or wooden wedge was driven in behind it to make as tight a fit against the barrel opening as could reasonably be expected, and the gun was fired. Breech-loaders were used in Europe from about 1370 onwards, and were most suitable for the smaller sizes of cannon. They were also a popular choice for naval warfare, because they did not need to be hauled in to be swabbed out and reloaded before being run out again for firing. The main disadvantage was leakage around the chamber and a consequent loss of explosive energy, but this was compensated for by a comparatively high rate of fire, as several breech containers could be prepared in advance.

The first east Asian country to acquire breech-loading cannon from Europe was China. They called the guns *folang zhi*, which means 'Frankish gun'. The 'Franks' was the general term for any inhabitants of the lands to the west. It was once believed that the first 'Frankish' piece came to China from Portugal via a shipwreck in 1523, but it is now believed that the transmission occurred some time earlier. The description of an early *folang zhi* notes that each weighed about 200 catties (264lbs, or 118kg). Its chambers, of which three were supplied for rotational use, weighed 30 catties (40lbs, or 18kg) each, and fired a small lead shot of 10oz (280g).

DISASTER AT THE MIMIGAWA

Breech-loading cannon entered Japan about half a century later under the name of *furangi*. Otomo Sôrin may have been the first recipient in 1551, although the reference is not entirely reliable, but they appear to have been used in the defence of the Otomo castle of Tachibana in Chikuzen province in 1569. We know far more about their use by Otomo Sôrin in 1578. By this time the Shimazu had been campaigning against the Otomo neighbours, the Ito family in Hyuga, for many years. Ito Yoshisuke finally capitulated in 1576, and sought refuge with Otomo Sôrin. This brought the Otomo and Shimazu territories closer together, a process that was completed when the final 'buffer *daimyo*', the Tsuchimochi family of northern Hyuga, betrayed the Otomo and declared for the Shimazu.

On 12 August 1578 the Otomo began to move south to challenge the Shimazu. Otomo Sôrin took personal command of 35,000 men and advanced into the disputed territory. He rapidly destroyed the rebel Tsuchimochi clan at their fortress of Agata. This sent a clear signal to the Shimazu about the Otomo capacity and desire for war. As he advanced his great army grew to 50,000 men. It was not long before the Otomo had advanced beyond the Mimigawa into Shimazu territory. On a rocky plateau ten miles (16km) to the south of the Mimigawa was the castle of Takajô. It was held on behalf of Shimazu Yoshihisa by his retainer Yamada Arinobu with a garrison of 500 men. On 20 October the Otomo set up camp on high ground to the east of the castle. Here they established a gun position and set up two large breech-loading cannon obtained from the Portuguese. Sôrin no doubt recalled the devastating effects of the bombardment of Moji, and his Christian connections now allowed the technique to be tried from land. The cannon were nicknamed *kunikuzushi* (destroyer of

A woodblock print showing an army emerging from a castle gate. The bridge is a solid ramp built over an earth core, just like the castle mound itself.

provinces), and a bombardment of Takajô castle soon began. The Otomo troops expected the siege to be a brief one.

The samurai in the Shimazu garrison at Takajô were hopelessly outnumbered and suffered under fire from these unfamiliar weapons. As true samurai they were prepared to die at their posts, but they were much encouraged by two events. The defenders were suffering from a shortage of drinking water. They had previously obtained water from a stream that ran outside the castle walls, but the Otomo had cut their means of access to it. Then one day, as if by a miracle, a spring appeared beneath the castle walls. The other miracle was the sudden arrival of the youngest Shimazu brother Iehisa with reinforcements. Shimazu Yoshihisa followed up his youngest brother's advance and prepared to meet the Otomo in battle. They had 30,000 men against the Otomo's 50,000. The night before the battle Shimazu Yoshihisa had a dream, as a result of which he composed a poem:

The enemy's defeated host
Is as the maple leaves of autumn,
Floating on the water
Of the Takuta stream.

This was naturally regarded as a good omen, and made known to the army.

When day dawned the Shimazu sent their vanguard on ahead while the rest of the army lay concealed from view. This was the classic Shimazu decoy tactic at its best. In the centre was the experienced Shimazu Yoshihiro as the decoy force, while his relatives Shimazu Tadahira and Shimazu Tadamune were prepared to attack from the sides. Shimazu Yoshihisa provided the reserve from his headquarters unit on a hill to the rear. In a skilled application of the false withdrawal they allowed the Otomo troops to attack their centre, which held the impact of the assault, and then moved into a controlled retreat. The Shimazu withdrew back across the river, leading the Otomo on. Then the troops concealed on the flank moved in, catching the Otomo on the same bank of the river. Finally, Shimazu Iehisa and Yamada Arinobu sallied out from Takajô castle to attack them at the rear. The result was a disaster for Otomo Sôrin. Three of his generals were killed along with thousands of samurai and *ashigaru* who lay strewn along the banks of the Mimigawa. Shimazu Yoshihisa's poetic dream had come horribly true, because near to the Mimigawa were two large ponds. Many of the Otomo died in these ponds, and the flags floating in the water looked like fallen maple leaves.

CANNON AT SHIMABARA

When the Shimazu scoured the Mimigawa battlefield after their victory they must have found the two cannon named *kunikuzushi*. Surprisingly, they do not seem to have carried them off as trophies, because we read of one of the same two cannon, or perhaps an identical model, being used against the Shimazu in their next encounter at Usuki in 1586. Even more surprising, this further use of a cannon seems to have had a devastating effect on the morale of the Shimazu, who by now were no strangers to cannon fire, even though they do not seem to have adopted the weapons themselves.

Two years earlier in 1584 they had seen the effects of cannon when they helped the Arima clan win the battle of Okita-Nawate. Shimazu Yoshihisa had sent a force of 3,000 soldiers under Shimazu Iehisa across Shimabara Bay to the peninsula of Shimabara. Taking the bait, Ryûzôji Takanobu marched down to Shimabara at the head of 50,000 men, and the two sides met in a fierce battle about one mile (1.6km) north of Shimabara in March 1584.

The Shimazu and Arima forces closed off the approaches to Shimabara by building a brushwood palisade that stretched down to the sea, while a hastily erected but very solid wooden gate gave access to the actual road. The land around was swampy, so the Shimazu were well protected. Their intentions were to operate the Shimazu trademark of a false retreat. The Shimazu centre was held by Shimazu Iehisa, while a detached Shimazu force lay concealed in the woods on the landward side. The Arima role was to provide flank support in the shape of a floating gunnery line of 30 men in each of 13 boats. They kept up a fierce fire against the Ryûzôji from offshore with heavy-calibre arquebuses and two cannon that were almost certainly breech-loading swivel guns like the Otomo's prize possessions. As Arima Harunobu was a Christian *daimyo*, the engagement attracted the attention of the Jesuit Luis Frois, who described the bombardment in the words:

The rhythm to which they kept was really something to see. First of all, reverently kneeling down with their hands towards heaven, they began reciting, 'Our Father which art in heaven, hallowed be thy name …' The first phase of the strategy being thus completed, they turned impatiently to load the cannon balls, and fired with such force against the enemy that with only one shot the whole sky could be seen to be filled with limbs. They fell on their knees once more. The petitions of the Sunday oration followed and in this way they inflicted heavy losses on the pagans, who lacked the courage to advance.

In spite of the casualties from the Arima guns, Ryûzôji had drawn the conclusion that the Shimazu force in the centre was small enough to be overcome easily. Waving his war fan, he led an advance down the road against the gate in the palisade to the accompaniment of loud war cries. At that point Shimazu Iehisa flung open the gate on the Shimabara road, and the Satsuma samurai closed in on them. They burst through three ranks of the Ryûzôji and reached Takanobu's bodyguard, who were powerless to save their lord.

THE SIEGE OF USUKI

The death of Ryûzôji Takanobu meant that there was one less *daimyo* in Kyûshû to oppose the seemingly unstoppable rise of the Shimazu, and in 1586 they turned their attentions once more to the Otomo. This latest attack was directed against Otomo Sôrin's headquarters castle of Usuki in Bungo. Usuki was an island castle, and in place of the sloping stone walls that one associates with Japanese fortress design Usuki's base was a large lump of solid rock just off the mainland. Sheer cliffs provided its walls, and a sandbar at low tide provided its only connection with the land. Nowadays land reclamation and the silting-up of the river mean that the ruins of Usuki castle sit on a plateau in the middle of the town.

The operation against Usuki involved three of the Shimazu brothers: Yoshihisa, Yoshihiro and Iehisa. Their vanguard advanced to a position where woods concealed their final movements from the view from the castle. Within the castle itself great hopes were laid on their Portuguese breech-loading cannon called *kunikuzushi*, which was being used to defend a fortress for the first time. It was mounted near the main gate on a stone platform that allowed a clear field of fire over the narrow stretch of sea and on to the dry land beyond. We are told that the samurai in charge of the gun was called Takemiya Musashi-no-kami, who proceeded to use *kunikuzushi* against the likely position where the Shimazu were lurking. He first placed one *kanme* (8.5lbs, or 3.8kg) of gunpowder into the detachable breech, then in addition to a lead cannonball he put in some smaller balls. The cannon was fired and the shot hit the grove of willow trees where the Shimazu

This is a replica of the heavy bronze breech-loading swivel gun nicknamed *kunikuzushi* 'destroyer of provinces' that defended the Otomo's castle of Usuki against the Shimazu attack.

troops lay concealed. Beneath the splintered branches soon lay many dead and wounded Satsuma samurai. The Shimazu were shaken by this unexpected development, but regained their composure sufficiently to mount an assault. This was beaten off, and soon the operation deteriorated into a stalemate. We may presume that the cannon was used many times, because eventually the Shimazu withdrew.

It is interesting to note from the above account that the Shimazu had brought along nothing comparable with which to batter down the walls of Usuki. Such siege tactics are almost completely absent from the Japanese scene until the siege of Osaka in 1614. In the field of Far Eastern siege warfare, Japan was very much the odd man out, because in continental east Asia a progression from siege crossbows through traction trebuchets to siege cannon was used for the primary purpose of battering down the walls of fortified towns. In Japan, with no tradition of walled cities, and mountain-top castles made of wood, siege machines were primarily either incendiary weapons using fire arrows, or anti-personnel devices.

The last appearance of breech-loading swivel guns was during the siege of Osaka in 1614. Their presence within the walls of Osaka castle served to illustrate how impoverished Toyotomi Hideyori was compared to the Tokugawa army outside. Hideyori's pathetic *furangi* guns could scarcely reach beyond the limits of their own outer defences, while the fire from the Tokugawa's muzzle-loading European culverins and sakers blasted even Osaka's keep from an unchallenged distance.

Notwithstanding their decisive contribution to samurai warfare, we may conclude this chapter by noting that firearms of all sizes were received in Japan both as a blessing and a curse. This was exactly the same ambivalent attitude towards them that was being expressed within Europe. Firearms helped a general win battles, but there was a cost that was measured not merely in men's lives. Honour, pride and personal glory were also placed under threat by these new weapons, whether that pride was possessed by a Spanish knight or a Japanese samurai.

The attitude that both cultures had in common was snobbery – these devilish weapons were usually operated by the lower classes of society. Arquebus balls, fired by unspeakable fellows no doubt, cut short the lives and careers of several notable knightly personalities of 16-century Europe, including the celebrated French knight, Bayard, and the Dutch commander, Louis of Nassau. We must therefore be grateful that none of the scores of Turkish bullets fired during the battle of Lepanto in 1571 struck home against the person of Don Miguel de Cervantes. Instead he survived to bring us Don Quixote, the fictional knight whose role as a symbol for the decline of knightly values in the face of artillery sums up the attitude that contemporary Europe shared with Japan. No Japanese account can quite equal the torrent of hatred against guns that Cervantes puts into the mouth of his 'ill-made knight':

Blessed were the times which lacked the dreadful fury of those diabolical engines, the artillery, whose inventor I firmly believe is now receiving the reward for his devilish invention in hell; an invention which allows a base and cowardly hand to take the life of a brave knight, in such a way that, without knowing how or why, when his valiant heart is full of courage, there comes some random shot – discharged perhaps by a man who fled in terror from the flash the accursed machine made in firing – and puts an end in a moment to the consciousness of one who deserved to enjoy life for many an age.

The cannon called *kunikuzushi*, which was being used to defend a fortress for the first time, was mounted near the main gate of Usuki castle on this stone platform that allowed a clear field of fire over the narrow stretch of sea and on to the dry land beyond. We are told that the samurai in charge of the gun was called Takemiya Musashi-no-kami, who proceeded to use *kunikuzushi* against the likely position where the Shimazu were lurking. The cannon was fired and the shot hit the grove of willow trees where the Shimazu troops lay concealed.

These sentiments are echoed in Yamamoto Tsunetomo's *Hagakure*. Here a similar pain at losing a gallant samurai from something so anonymous as a musket ball has to be inferred from the text, but is strongly indicated:

On the first day of the attack on Hara castle, Tsuruta Yashichibei went as a messenger from Lord Mimasaka to Oki Hyobu, but as he was delivering the message, he was shot through the pelvic region by a bullet fired from the castle and instantly fell on his face. He got up again and delivered the rest of the message, but was felled a second time. And died. Yashichibei's body was carried back by Taira Chihyoei. When Chihyoei was returning to Hyobu's camp, he too was struck by a musket ball and died.

CHAPTER SIX

Shields of stone

Matsumoto castle must rank as one of the most beautiful military buildings in the world. The original keep dates from 1597. The red bridge sets it off quite perfectly.

The siege and subsequent battle of Nagashino in 1575 together make up one of the pivotal events in samurai history. It began unremarkably. The army of Takeda Katsuyori had invaded Tokugawa Ieyasu's Mikawa province, and being frustrated by their primary objective, laid siege instead to the tiny but stubbornly defended fortress of Nagashino. The siege, which lasted nearly ten days, was a classic of the old style, conducted against a traditional castle built mainly from wood with some stone. Included in its defence were a modest number of arquebuses and only one cannon. Attacks upon it involved an assault party on a raft floated down the river, mining on the landward side, fire arrows loosed against the wooden buildings, but, above all, repeated assaults on the walls involving hand-to-hand fighting.

Oda Nobunaga, the powerful neighbouring *daimyo* who was destined to rise to great heights, sent an army to relieve Nagashino. When the relieving army arrived the Takeda abandoned their siege lines to give battle. The great strength of the Takeda was the immense striking power of their mounted samurai, but when the horsemen swept down upon the enemy lines they found themselves faced by 3,000 arquebusiers. The men had been trained to fire in organised volleys and were protected by a loose palisade. The gunfire broke the impact of the initial charge and, as the second wave of horsemen prepared to go in, the gunners calmly reloaded under the protection of their spearmen. Once again the line held, and when the Takeda faltered for a third time the samurai and footsoldiers of the Oda began to engage the attackers in hand-to-hand fighting. Several hours of conflict followed, at the end of which the Takeda withdrew after taking enormous numbers of casualties, broken for ever as a military and political influence in Japan.

The brief transition between the siege of Nagashino being temporarily abandoned and the battle of Nagashino beginning, a period of time lasting but a few hours, marks an important turning point in the development of samurai warfare. The conduct of the siege itself had been no different from hundreds of other similar operations elsewhere in Japan. By contrast, the battle that followed a few hours afterwards was the herald of a military revolution. A straightforward cavalry charge, the sort that had given the Takeda their victory at Mikata ga hara in 1572, was stunted by what was in effect a new type of field fortress that combined organised gunfire on a large scale with simple defence works. From this point on, Japanese warfare, in particular defensive warfare, would never be quite the same again, and when the Period of Warring States came to an end it left behind a legacy of fortresses that provide tantalising parallels with Europe, but can be shown to be based on very different principles and with very different intentions. In castle design, as with armour and weapons, Japan once again held up a mirror to the rest of the world.

THE EVOLUTION OF THE JAPANESE CASTLE

The type of Japanese castle that Nagashino represented already had a long history. As the Japanese landscape has always had a shortage of stone and an abundance of trees clustered on mountains, it was natural that it should be the latter two factors – timber and high ground – that determined the character of Japanese fortifications for many centuries. The first Japanese castles consisted of simple wooden stockades between towers and gates that followed the natural defences provided by the height and the contours of the mountains from which the materials for the wooden walls had been taken. The erection of palisades on top of earthworks, raised by excavating a forward ditch, could compensate for the lack of high ground when a position had to be erected in an area of flatlands, but such topography was avoided wherever possible. It was from the mountain-top

yamashiro (mountain castles) of Akasaka and Chihaya that Kusunoki Masashige conducted his spirited defensive campaigns and guerrilla actions on behalf of Emperor Go Daigo between 1331 and 1336.

Such designs persisted into the Period of Warring States. The *daimyo* led armies and ruled territories whose borders were defined solely by their latest conquests, and to defend their lands they adopted the *yamashiro* model on a huge scale. From one *honjo* (headquarters castle), a network of satellite castles radiated out, each of which had its own smaller sub-satellite, with each sub-satellite having its own local cluster of tiny guard posts. The network would often also be linked visually by a chain of fire beacons.

For a *daimyo's honjo*, and for most of the satellite castles, a simple stockade soon proved to be insufficient to withstand enemy attack or to provide barracks space for a large garrison, so a technique developed whereby the mountain on which the *yamashiro* stood was literally carved up. Using the formidable resources in manpower that successful *daimyo* could now command, neighbouring mountains were sculpted into a series of interlocking baileys. They followed the natural lines only in the sense that the contours provided the guide for the excavation of wide, flat horizontal surfaces, each overlooked by the one above it. The result was a gigantic and complex mound produced by removing materials rather than piling them up. On top of the site were placed fences, towers, stables, storehouses, walkways, bridges, gates and usually a rudimentary version of a castle keep. Very little stone was used in the construction except for strengthening the bases of gatehouses and towers and to combat soil erosion from the excavated slopes. As time went by the simple palisades and towers inside the *yamashiro* were replaced by stronger wattle and daub walls, plastered over against fire attack and roofed with tiles as a protection against rain.

By the time of the battle of Nagashino it had also been realised that much larger, taller and heavier buildings could be successfully raised on top of the *yamashiro* if the cut-away slopes of the natural hills were reinforced with tightly packed stones. The sloping stone surfaces were designed mathematically so that

Iwakuni castle, on the forested hill beyond the river, provides a good example of a *yamashiro* site, where the castle is on top of a mountain. The famous bridge called the Kintai-kyo (the brocade sash bridge) dates from 1673 and originally only members of the samurai class could cross it. Townspeople had to take a ferry.

RIGHT AND OPPOSITE Nothing shows the strength of a stone-clad Japanese castle mound more than these 'before' and 'after' pictures of Hiroshima castle. The graceful superstructure has gone, but even the atomic bomb in 1945 could not make much impression on the stone base.

any weight upon them was dissipated outwards and downwards. This took the extra weight, and also provided a cushion against earth tremors. In addition to cutting away existing hills, similar artificial mounds were built in this way on flat areas and encased with stone. On top of the stone-clad mounds were raised primitive versions of the castle keeps that are now such an attractive feature of extant Japanese military architecture.

It is unlikely that little Nagashino possessed a keep in any form other than a simple two-storey wooden building with a Japanese-style curving roof, but in one respect Nagashino castle was exceptionally fortunate. It was not built upon a stripped-out mountain, but very literally founded on solid rock in the form of a dramatic promontory that marked the confluence of two minor rivers that joined at Nagashino to become the mighty

Toyokawa. These rocky cliffs formed two sides of an equilateral triangle, which was completed on its third side by an outer bailey of a simple ditch, mound and palisade construction.

This combination of two impregnable rocky sides and the sheer determination of the defenders behind the wall of the third side kept every ingenious Takeda attack at bay, so Takeda Katsuyori settled down for what could be a long wait until the defenders surrendered from starvation. But then the situation changed. A brave warrior called Torii Sune'emon slipped out of the castle and took a message to Oda Nobunaga, who immediately set out with a relieving army. But Nobunaga did not simply fall precipitately onto the rear of the Takeda lines. Instead, he halted on a low ridge a few miles away. It had a forest to its rear and left, a stream in front, and a river to its right. With the aid of wooden stakes and the massed ranks of his gunners Nobunaga converted the site into an instant castle. The battle of Nagashino was therefore won not from behind the walls of a fortress but from a simple position constructed overnight and defended by guns. Nobunaga's victory showed the effectiveness of something that had been created both temporarily and quickly.

CASTLES AND THE NAGASHINO EFFECT

The 'Nagashino effect' was disseminated quite rapidly throughout Japan because the roll call of Oda Nobunaga's army included many of the men who were to be enormously influential in the following years. Toyotomi Hideyoshi, Tokugawa Ieyasu and Shibata Katsuie are but three of the movers and shakers of Japanese history who fought shoulder to shoulder at Nagashino. They went on to fight each other having learned the lessons of Nagashino at first hand.

When the battle of Nagashino ended, Oda Nobunaga returned to his base at Gifu with much unfinished business on his hands. At the top of the agenda was the final destruction of the warrior monks of the Ikkô-ikki, whose early adoption of firearms had been a precursor to Nagashino. It was Nobunaga himself who had experienced at their hands the effects of the mass use of arquebuses during an attack on their fortified cathedral of Ishiyama Honganji. This, combined with Nobunaga's own earlier

OPPOSITE An excellent reconstruction of a wooden lookout tower appears here at the Ise Sengoku village. An *ashigaru* mounts guard, and extra protection is provided by removable wooden shields.

Hagi castle mound is all that remains of the castle that was the headquarters of the Chôshû *han*. It nevertheless shows the principle behind the design of Japanese castles around a sturdy earthen base, often carved out of a hillside, clad in strong stone blocks.

experiments with rotating volleys, had led directly to his battlefield layout at Nagashino. Over the next few years the newly confident Nobunaga literally met fire with fire, and finally overcame the warrior monks in 1580. Meanwhile Takeda Katsuyori, the loser at Nagashino, showed what a lesson that battle had been for him by making a major strategic U-turn. For half a century the Takeda had won and controlled territory without ever building anything that could be described as a castle. Tsutsujigasaki, the Takeda capital, was a mansion built on flat ground with little more than a moat and a fence for protection. But as Nobunaga's armies closed in on his home province Katsuyori abandoned Tsutsujigasaki for the stone walls of newly built Shimpu. His retainers saw it as a very bad omen, a prophecy that came true with Katsuyori's defeat and death in 1582.

In 1583 Oda Nobunaga's successor Toyotomi Hideyoshi was to be found fighting his former Nagashino comrade-in-arms Sakuma Morimasa at the battle of Shizugatake. Morimasa had besieged the mountain fortress of Shizugatake, which, like Nagashino, was holding out stubbornly. Hideyoshi was informed that Morimasa had not abandoned his siege lines for the security of one of the *yamashiro* that he had successfully captured. This provided the opportunity for him to be surprised, so Toyotomi Hideyoshi advanced on Shizugatake in a rapid forced march. Sakuma Morimasa's position was Nagashino in reverse. Expecting no response from Hideyoshi for several days he had stayed in the unprotected siege lines. Hideyoshi fell upon him before he had a chance to erect any form of field fortifications, and soon his entire army was defeated.

Such a failure to benefit from the first-hand experience of Nagashino was not shared by Tokugawa Ieyasu, who was the next rival to challenge Hideyoshi for supremacy. Their territories met in Owari province, and it was the way in which their antagonism was resolved that was to show the most dramatic influence from the Nagashino effect. Owari province was largely flatland, so Ieyasu took the opportunity to secure one of the few pieces of high ground. This was the site of the former castle of Komaki, 300 feet (27m) above sea level. As time was pressing, Ieyasu's men took to the spade and raised earth ramparts as Komaki's defences in a few days. Four other forts were also strengthened to provide secure communications to the south and west.

Hideyoshi soon heard of Ieyasu's activities and responded in kind. Neither of his two front-line forts of Iwasakiyama and Nijubori had Komaki's advantage of high ground, so, with memories of Nagashino behind him, he ordered the construction of a long rampart to join the two together. The resulting earthwork, probably strengthened with wood, was completed overnight. It was over a mile long, 12 feet (3.5m) high and seven feet (2m) thick, and was pierced with several gates to allow a counter-attack. The slope of the rampart no doubt also allowed for the provision of firing positions. Satisfied with his Nagashino-like front line, Hideyoshi set up his headquarters to the rear at Gakuden. The following morning, upon observing Hideyoshi's rampart, Ieyasu immediately ordered a similar line to be constructed parallel to it and out from Komaki to the south-east. This was a more modest construction only half a mile (0.8km) long and anchored on the small fort of Hachimanzuka, from where it was a short distance to his communications forts of Hira and Kobata. The result was that two veterans of Nagashino

This view of Osaka's walls shows how a long wall could be concertinaed into a design known as *byobu* (folding screen). This allowed for the important element of heavy flanking fire from hundreds of arquebuses. The huge stone walls seem to dwarf the great keep of Osaka that appears in the distance.

were now facing each other from behind the 16th-century equivalent of a World War I trench system.

It was almost inevitable that the lessons of Nagashino should not only have caused these highly skilled generals to take the above defensive measures, but should also prevent either of them from making the first move in attacking each other. The result was an inevitable stalemate, which was not a situation at all conducive to the samurai spirit. So within a few days there occurred the bloody but indecisive battle of Nagakute. However, Nagakute was not fought between the Komaki lines, but several miles away. It arose from an attempt by one of Hideyoshi's generals to raid Ieyasu's home province while he was sitting in the ramparts of Komaki. When Nagakute had been fought (with considerable casualties), both armies returned to their lines, and the stalemate began again. Once more boredom set in, and this time it was relieved by Hideyoshi withdrawing more men to besiege Ieyasu's ally Oda Nobuo in his castle of Kagenoi. In fact no frontal attack between the two ever took place at Komaki, and eventually their differences were settled by negotiation. The ramparts were then allowed to crumble back into the rice fields.

EARTHWORKS IN KOREA

The next example of the use of earthworks combined with guns is to be found during Hideyoshi's invasion of Korea in 1592. The rapid advance of the Japanese up the Korean peninsula stalled following the capture of P'yongyang. P'yongyang had been defended by stone walls that were very different from the Japanese model. They were not based round an earth core but were of the usual Korean pattern of a long, vertical but narrow construction. There were walkways at the tops of the walls and battlements, and several strong stone gateways. Such walls resembled the Great Wall of China, but proved very vulnerable to the Japanese tactic of using assault parties.

P'yongyang thus passed into Japanese hands, but when the city came under threat from the expeditionary army sent by Ming China the Japanese defenders made no attempt to increase the size of the Korean walls. Instead they turned to the style of fortress they were used to, and began digging and shovelling earth and stones to augment the existing defences of the city by horizontal earthworks. P'yongyang therefore provides the first example of the construction of recognisable Japanese-style fortifications in Korea. The advancing Chinese, who compared the Japanese efforts unfavourably to their own magnificent Great Wall, scorned the crude ramparts, referring to them as 'earth caverns', and likened them to the primitive earthworks found among the Jurchids of Manchuria. What the Chinese did not realise was that these 'earth caverns' were designed to provide a clear field of fire for thousands of arquebuses and to absorb whatever punishment the Chinese cannon could throw

Being set back from the road, the gate of Takamatsu castle shows such a feature very much as it would have appeared during the 16th century. At high tide the sea moat laps at the walls, so at low tide we have a very good impression of an old muddy street. Note the gun and arrow ports, the defensive areas and the tiled roofs.

at them. The attack came in the winter, by which time the earthworks were frozen solid around their absorbent core. The Chinese cannon balls sank in without doing much harm, while the samurai defended their frozen ramparts as if they were made of stone.

In 1614 Japan was again to see an earthwork play a vital role during the Winter Campaign of Osaka. When Toyotomi Hideyori repaired and enlarged his late father's castle at Osaka, an important addition to the forward defences was provided in the form of a barbican earthwork called the Sanada-maru after its commander Sanada Yukimura. In front of the Sanada-maru was a wide ditch with palisades on either side and one along the middle of the base. There were wooden towers and walls with a two-storey firing platform, and the whole complex bristled with guns. Even though little if any stone was used in its construction the Sanada-maru held out against one of the first and fiercest attacks of the siege of Osaka.

NOBUNAGA AND AZUCHI

The graceful castle towers that we see today at places such as Himeji and Matsumoto are the most beautiful survivors from the world of the warrior. They are also the direct descendants of Oda Nobunaga's other contribution to military architecture. The use of earthworks defended by massed arquebuses is one of Oda Nobunaga's legacies to defensive warfare. There is also one other, because within a year of the battle of Nagashino this same talented general would also be demonstrating the effectiveness of the opposite extreme in castle design where huge stone walls enclosed a massive keep.

In 1576 Japan was to see the first, and perhaps the finest, of a new style of permanent military bases and palaces combined in one castle building. This was Nobunaga's castle of Azuchi, which demonstrated his power in several ways. First, its design showed the culmination of the technique of encasing the excavated hills of a *yamashiro* in shaped and cut stone. No bare earthen walls were now visible. All were made from graceful sloping stone and, as well as providing their own defences, these cyclopean mounds above a core of bedrock allowed the raising of a spectacular seven-storey keep ornamented within and without as befitted the grandeur to which Nobunaga aspired. Around Azuchi's central keep were a score of smaller towers, each of which would have done credit as the main keep for a normal-sized castle. Azuchi was huge, and could therefore house an enormous garrison that few *daimyo* could afford either to feed or to arm. Nobunaga could do both, and the internal walls of Azuchi were fitted with numerous racks for hundreds of arquebuses that could be quickly lifted down and poked out through the windows and weapon slits of the towers. The towers were also cunningly designed to enable flanking fire to be delivered from neighbouring sections.

Azuchi castle never had to withstand a siege, and in fact its end was ignominious. Nobunaga was murdered in 1582 when he was away from Azuchi on campaign and, with its master and army gone, the mighty edifice was raided and burned to the ground. But its example had served its purpose. Castle builders now knew that size mattered. In 1586 Hideyoshi built Osaka castle with a large keep inside perimeter walls 12 miles (19km) in circumference.

This view of the interior of Uwajima castle was taken looking down from the central stairwell. The room is enclosed by sliding screens, while the wooden floor outside provides the main means of getting round the floors.

With the fall of the Hôjô in 1590 Tokugawa Ieyasu acquired their fortress of Edo and set about extending it to create the mightiest castle in the land. It is now the Imperial Palace in Tokyo.

Like all the extant Japanese fortresses, Osaka no longer possesses in its entirety the original massive complex of outer works. These once stretched so far that the massive keeps we enjoy today could then have been seen from only a distance. For this reason it is difficult to assess their design from a military perspective. It is therefore important to realise that the fundamental defining feature of a Japanese castle was not its ornate keep but the huge overlapping walls made from the carved stone-clad hillsides. The earliest tower keeps date only from the 1570s, and many were not added to the existing complex of smaller towers until early in the 17th century. It can also be shown from sources such as painted screens of battle exploits that the majority of the keeps that withstood attack during the time of civil wars would have been of much simpler construction than these magnificent towers. Without these encircling walls, Himeji's keep, for example, looks very vulnerable, until one realises that for an attacker to take on that graceful tower he would have had to fight through a series of formidable baileys, all of which have since disappeared. It is only when these walls are put back using one's imagination that a useful assessment may be made. When this is done several interesting and instructive parallels may be noted with contemporary Europe.

JAPANESE CASTLES AND THE EUROPEAN PARALLEL

In medieval Europe the trend in castle-building had been to build up the curtain walls as high as possible so that an assailant's siege towers and scaling ladders would have to be impossibly long. It also meant that stones from trebuchets would strike at an angle too acute to do much damage. But when cannon were introduced it became possible to deliver a destructive missile on a flatter trajectory that would hit a wall at nearly 90 degrees. High medieval walls were therefore very vulnerable to cannon fire. One solution was to add width to height, so that European fortresses grew into enormous complexes. A simpler remedy was to pile up earth behind the walls or inside towers to increase their thickness.

Unfortunately, when breaches were made the earth that fell out provided an easy slope for an assailant to climb. This problem was solved with the introduction of the model of low, squat and very thick walls. The lower walls, of course, made assault that much easier, so, instead of high corner towers, lower, angled bastions were introduced from where fire could be directed along the flanks of the building against scaling parties, leaving no blind spots.

This was the castle design that became known in Europe as the *trace italienne*, the size of its ditches and walls and the deployment of sharpshooters with arquebuses keeping a besiegers' own artillery as far away as possible. To surround a European city with the elaborate and mathematically intricate *trace italienne* castles built of stone was a very expensive undertaking, so many used the same design but employed earth instead. As in the Japanese experience in Korea and at Osaka these were found to have the advantage of both speed and cost, and provided a deep area of absorbency for cannon shot.

The Japanese experience provides a parallel, but with some curious differences. Japanese castle technology, prior to the introduction of the tower keep in the 1570s, did not allow the use of height as a defence except for the natural height of the hill that was provided by nature through the *yamashiro* model. The Japanese certainly went for width as another means of keeping an enemy at bay when they joined neighbouring hills together in a complex of encircling baileys. With the introduction of stone, projecting towers and walls were added to the Japanese castle and were referred to picturesquely as *koguchi* (tigers' mouths). Alternatively, or in addition, a long wall could be concertinaed into a design known as *byobu* (folding screen). Both allowed the important element of heavy flanking fire from hundreds of arquebuses. In front of the European bastions would be a wide ditch, just as in many Japanese examples, with a slope (the European *glacis*) running down towards the besiegers' lines.

This European technique of low and squat fortresses whose stone walls were packed behind with earth thus looks remarkably similar to the Japanese designs that used the same technique in reverse by excavating a mountain and encasing it in stone. However, even though the Japanese stone-clad mounds look

OPPOSITE This illustration is provided for comparison between Japanese and European styles. This is the Bastion St André at Montmedy, designed by the famous Vauban. The similarity with a Japanese castle wall is quite striking, but in fact they were originally designed in this way for two different reasons. Both, however, allow the clear field of fire across the flanks.

A corner tower of Osaka castle shows the angle of the stone-clad base. The edges are neatly arranged using huge dressed stones.

identical to the European bastions, they were built for totally different reasons. The Japanese style evolved out of the *yamashiro* model in a situation where there were few heavy guns to worry about, while the European model was designed specifically to counter just that threat. As the previous chapter suggested, if Japan had possessed heavy artillery during the Period of Warring States then the pattern that emerged of castles being defended by hundreds of arquebuses rather than one or two big guns may have been very different. However, it is worth noting that for a gun to destroy one of the stone mounds built around an excavated mountain it would have had to be very powerful indeed. Proof of this is provided by the experience of Hiroshima castle in August 1945. All the superstructure of the castle disappeared in the atomic blast, but the great stone-clad mound survived almost unscathed.

JAPANESE CASTLES IN KOREA

As noted above, we have to envisage a contemporary Japanese castle either without its tower keep or with many other encircling walls if we are to appreciate the reality of siege warfare at the end of the Period of Warring States. This is not always easy to do in Japan itself, but good examples may be found in Korea – during the invasion of 1592–98 the Japanese established a chain of coastal fortresses called *wajo* to protect their communications with Japan. As the *wajo* never had the tower keeps that were added later to Japanese castles, their remains provide useful information about contemporary castle design and allow a direct comparison with European models.

The example quoted above of the use of earthworks at the siege of P'yongyang showed a temporary response to a situation that was to acquire permanence through the *wajo*. Instead of the Chinese and Korean 'Great Wall' styles of walls snaking up and down the mountains, we see the more labour-intensive Japanese model of large-scale excavations to provide horizontal surfaces and the use of carefully designed sloping walls rather than the simpler Korean walls of flat stone. Some castles had to be built very quickly, and thousands of Japanese labourers were shipped over to help with construction work, where they joined many thousands more captive Koreans. At Ulsan even the walls and gateways were incomplete as the Ming forces advanced upon it in the winter of 1597, and an eyewitness recorded the brutality meted out by the commanders to the Korean and Japanese labourers impressed to the task. Earthworks and palisades added to the hasty defences where there was no time to build with stone, and a chronicler noted how it gave the illusion that the third bailey was complete. When the Chinese attacks began many samurai were still encamped outside the unfinished walls.

The main reason why the invaders spurned the native style of fortress design for their more permanent constructions was the fact that nearly all the resistance put up inside Korean castles from Pusan to P'yongyang had collapsed before the initial Japanese advance, spearheaded by volleys from massed ranks of gunners. The coastal location for the *wajo* commanded excellent visibility out to sea and a well-defended anchorage that could in some way be linked securely to the fortress on the hill behind. The best example of this is Sunch'on, which is very well preserved. The whole area is still exactly as it was once the mountain had been scooped away and the stone facings added.

When the Chinese launched their attacks on the *wajo* the theory held good and the combination of gunfire covering every angle of a simple but solid series of walls meant that the Japanese did not lose a single one of their castles. The attack on Sach'on provides an excellent illustration. There were two castles at Sach'on. The 'old castle' was a Korean fortress taken over by the Japanese, while the 'new castle' was a *wajo* built on a promontory two miles to the south-west, where it overlooked the harbour and provided a safe anchorage. It was defended by Shimazu Yoshihiro and his son, Tadatsune. In preparation for their attack on Sach'on, the Chinese army advanced as far as Chinju. When four outposts were lost to the Chinese, young Shimazu Tadatsune was all for making an immediate attack, but his father forbade it. He reasoned that the Chinese army would wish to waste no time in attacking, and that the men of Satsuma were ready for them in their *wajo*. This assumption proved to be correct, and the Ming army moved in for an attack at about 6.00 am on 30 October 1598 with a total of 36,700 troops. The Shimazu father and son monitored their movements from the two towers that flanked the eastern gate.

Under strict orders from Yoshihiro, the Japanese held their fire, and as one or two men fell dead from Chinese arrows, Tadatsune was again for launching an attack, but once more his father urged caution.

By now the Chinese were approaching the walls, and were also attacking the main gate with a curious siege engine that combined an iron-tipped battering ram with a cannon. The joint effects of cannonball and ram smashed the gate, and soon thousands of Chinese soldiers were fighting at the entrance and climbing up the castle walls. 'Lord Yoshihiro, who saw this, gave the order to attack without delay,' writes a commentator on behalf of the Shimazu, 'and all the soldiers as one body fired their arquebuses and mowed down the enemy soldiers who were clinging on to the walls.' At this precise moment the Japanese managed to destroy the combined ram and cannon, causing its stock of gunpowder to explode with great fury right in the middle of the Ming host. A separate Shimazu chronicle implies that the engine was destroyed by a fire bomb thrown from a mortar or a catapult, because:

We flung fire against the gunpowder jars, many of which had been placed within the enemy ranks. It flew from one jar to another, and the tremendous noise was carried to our ears. Consequently the alarming sound terrified all the enemy who were in the vicinity.

This dramatic moment proved to be the turning point of the battle. Seeing the confusion in the Chinese ranks, Shimazu Yoshihiro led out his men in a tremendous charge. Many Chinese were cut down, but showing admirable organisation and discipline the army regrouped on a nearby hill and took the fight back to the Japanese. Some Japanese units had now become detached from the main body, and the Shimazu remained outnumbered by three to one until the approach of a relieving army from the nearest *wajo* at Kosong tipped the balance in Japan's favour. Thousands of Chinese were killed or pursued back as far as the Nam river, where very few stragglers managed to cross and reach the safety of Chinju. Sach'on was China's worst defeat

at Japanese hands. The site is now marked by a massive burial mound containing the remains of more than 30,000 Ming troops killed by the Japanese and interred here without their noses. Those trophies were taken back to Japan as proof of duty done, and lie to this day within the erroneously named 'Ear Mound' in Kyôto.

The overall progress of the war and the death of Hideyoshi meant that the *wajo* ended up being purely defensive structures to cover the Japanese withdrawal rather than as the outposts of empire. Had things gone differently then the *wajo* might well have represented a parallel with the coastal forts of the Europeans, who established garrisons defended by artillery at places like Mombasa, Havana and Manila to serve as bases

One of the best examples of the *wajo*, the castles built by the Japanese in Korea, is Sunch'on, which is very well preserved. The whole area is still exactly as it was once the mountain had been scooped away and the stone facings added. When the Chinese launched their attacks on the *wajo* the combination of gunfire covering every angle of a simple but solid series of walls meant that the Japanese did not lose a single one of their castles.

for overseas expansion and colonisation. Instead, the samurai returned home in defeat, and put into practice the lessons they had learned from the successful repulse of the huge assaults the Chinese had mounted on the *wajo*. The combination of wall and gun had held them off. In Korea the lessons learned at Nagashino and Azuchi had been subjected to their most searching test and had passed with flying colours.

LESSONS FROM KOREA

Within two years of their return from the Korean War the *daimyo* who had gone to fight abroad were to split into the two armed camps that brought about the decisive showdown at Sekigahara. A spate of castle-building followed, and one *daimyo* in particular demonstrated in his castle the lessons that he had learned in Korea. Katô Kiyomasa had become a hero by his defence of the *wajo* of Ulsan, and put all that experience into his designs for Kumamoto castle. The walls and towers were of course formidable, but he also planted nut trees inside the massive sloping stone walls to provide food during a siege. Wells were sunk, and in a curious gesture of preparation Kiyomasa ordered that the *tatami* (floor mats) inside the towers should be stuffed not with rice straw but with vegetable stalks so that a desperate garrison could literally eat the floor!

We will see in a later chapter how Katô Kiyomasa's ideas were tested in battle, but castles similar to Kumamoto were to be found in every province until, with the achievement of Tokugawa supremacy, the *daimyo* were ordered to demolish every castle in their territories except one. The resulting edifices, many of which still exist today, brought the evolution from sculpted mountain to military palace to a level of perfection in terms of architecture and military necessity. The development in castle design from mountain stockade to fortress of stone was therefore complete. It owed much to the initial confirmation of the power of guns in a fortified position that was demonstrated so powerfully for the first time on the bloody field of Nagashino and then transferred to a large canvas at Azuchi. Through these two elements the legacy of Oda Nobunaga lives on in the Japanese castles of today.

When rulers such as Toyotomi Hideyoshi and Tokugawa Ieyasu embarked upon major
castle-building programmes the *daimyo* vied with each other to supply massive stones for
the walls. This statue commemorates Katô Kiyomasa's gift of a big stone for Nagoya castle.

Azuchi castle, 1576. Only a stone base remains of the great Azuchi castle, raised by Oda Nobunaga in 1576 as one of the wonders of Japan. It was Japan's first great tower keep and was burned to the ground when Nobunaga was assassinated only six years later. For this reason no one can be sure for certain what Azuchi actually looked like, but the consensus of opinion is that this revolutionary building had seven storeys, of which the uppermost one was octagonal and richly decorated. Military corridors inside surrounded domestic areas. (Artwork by Peter Dennis)

CHAPTER SEVEN

Samurai with a pinch of salt

In 1168 Taira Kiyomori, whose family made their name by quelling pirates, showed his attachment to the sea by founding the Shintô shrine of Itsukushima on the island of Miyajima. The shrine is built upon wooden stilts over the beach, and when the tide is in the whole ensemble seems to be floating on the waves. This is the great *torii* (Shintô gateway) at high tide.

The samurai is not commonly thought of as a sea-going creature. Somehow the image of an elite mounted archer does not sit squarely on the deck of a ship, and even the great naval battle of Dan no Ura gives the impression that it was fought by warriors who were more at home on dry land. The later history of the samurai gives little more encouragement. The naval battles of the Period of Warring States were fought from ships so apparently clumsy that capsizing was as much a risk as enemy action, and the naval campaign of the Korean War proved as much an embarrassment as it did a disaster. Finally, the Closed Country Edict of the Tokugawa *bakufu* put a stop to nearly all mercantile endeavour until the time of the Meiji Restoration. It is hardly the picture of a seafaring nation.

All the above points are true as far as they go, and it may indeed be said that official samurai naval activity was very limited. But Japan has always had a naval tradition. The country itself consists of numerous islands, and both China and Korea are a comparatively short sea voyage away. With a lively internal seaborne trade and a strong fishing fleet, we should expect to see these activities replicated in the wartime operations of the samurai, and indeed we do. It is merely a question of looking in the right places. Some *daimyo* were as much lords of the sea as they were lords of the land, and there was military activity in plenty. It was simply carried out in a very unofficial capacity.

THE FIRST JAPANESE PIRATES

In an earlier chapter, reference was made to the rebels against the throne whose elimination provided rewards and prestige to the up-and-coming samurai clans of the Nara and Heian Periods. Not all of these rebels operated exclusively on dry land. In 939 a courtier called Fujiwara Sumitomo, who served as an official to the governor of Iyo province on Shikoku Island, was ordered to destroy the local pirates. Instead of suppressing them Sumitomo joined in with their activities and began marauding the coasts of the Inland Sea at the head of his own band of cut-throats. It took two years to catch him, and, in the end, this success coming largely because his second in command betrayed him by revealing his secret hiding places and storage areas. The final victory over Sumitomo was in Hakata Bay in Kyûshû. Sumitomo escaped in a small boat but was later captured in Iyo province and killed. His head was sent to Kyôtô for public display.

For the loyal warriors who held lands in south-western Japan, particularly around the coastline of the Inland Sea, the quelling of such pirates provided an opportunity for glory equivalent to the wars against the *emishi* practised by their contemporaries in the north-east. In fact the rise to power of the Taira family owed a great deal to their anti-piracy duties. Taira Tadamori (1096–1153) was granted an imperial commission to chastise pirates in 1129. The rewards made him rich but gave him many enemies, and Tadamori survived at least one assassination attempt. Tadamori's skills were inherited by his son Taira Kiyomori (1118–81), under whose leadership the Taira reached their greatest heights of power. When he wasn't fighting his enemies Kiyomori supervised the dredging of channels and the development of the area around modern Hiroshima to improve conditions for trade with China. In 1168 Kiyomori showed his family's attachment to the sea by founding the Shintô shrine of Itsukushima on the island of Miyajima. This is still one of Japan's greatest sights. The shrine is built upon wooden stilts over the beach, and when the tide is in the whole ensemble seems to be floating on the waves.

THE SCOURGE OF THE *WAKO*

The bitter irony of the defeat of the sea-going Taira in the greatest sea battle in Japanese history brought all activities by this family to an abrupt end. Although it is tempting to see the battle of Dan no Ura in 1185 as providing a respite for the pirates, their lairs were in any case many and their targets various. For example, far away in Hizen province (now Nagasaki prefecture) in north-west Kyûshû, hidden among coves, peninsulas and tiny islands, lurked a group of families known collectively as the Matsuura-*to*. They first became notorious during the 1220s for their pirate raids on Korea. The Koreans called the Japanese pirates *waegu*, which was rendered into Japanese as *wako*, the 'brigands from the country of Wa (i.e. Japan). In 1227 the Kyûshû representative of the Kamakura *bakufu* had 90 suspect *wako* beheaded in front of a Korean envoy. This greatly curtailed piratical activity. It also showed the control that Kamakura was able to exercise so many miles from its eastern heartlands, a control that was put to very good use when Japan was faced with the Mongol invasions of 1274 and 1281. Although best remembered for the death blow delivered by the *kamikaze* typhoon, the Mongol troops would not have been riding at anchor on their ships had the samurai not kept them there by their determination and bravery. Night after night boatloads of samurai were rowed out to the Mongol ships to engage their crews in hand-to-hand fighting. So persistent was the assault that no permanent landfall was made on the Japanese mainland before the *kamikaze* blew.

Matters changed again in the mid-14th century. The Hôjô regency was crumbling in the face of Go Daigo's rebellion, and the confusion of the Nanbokuchô Wars was as noticeable in Kyûshû as it was elsewhere in Japan. Supporters of the Southern Court fought supporters of the Northern Court and, while they squabbled the *wako* started their raids all over again. In addition to the disruption in Japanese politics, the situation in Korea was also favourable to raiding because the Koryo dynasty was on its last legs and was soon to be supplanted by the Choson dynasty. During the ten years between 1376 and 1385 there were 174 recorded *wako* raids on Korea. Some of these expeditions amounted to miniature Japanese invasions of Korea, with as many as 3,000 *wako* penetrating far from the coast, ravaging Kaesong, the Koryo capital, and even pillaging as far north as

OPPOSITE In 1389 a successful raid by Korea was carried out against pirates based on the Japanese island of Tsushima. This painting in the War Memorial in Seoul shows Japanese pirates kneeling before the raiders.

P'yongyang. In addition to looting property, the *wako* became slave-traders. Some bands of *wako* ravaged as far as China.

On several occasions the Korean navy hit back. In 1380 over 500 Japanese ships were set ablaze while three years later Admiral Chong Chi, in command of 47 ships, chased away more than 100 Japanese with gunfire. In 1389 a successful raid by Korea was carried out against pirates based on the Japanese island of Tsushima, but the most important influence against the *wako* was political. In 1392 Japan acquired a new shogun. His name was Ashikaga Yoshimitsu, and in addition to the achievements for which he is best known – the reconciliation between the rival Southern and Northern Courts and the building of the Kinkakuji or Golden Pavilion in Kyôto – Yoshimitsu proved to be a great queller of pirates. As in so much of his career, Ashikaga Yoshimitsu won his battles by political means. Because the Ming emperor regarded the rest of the entire world as members of a universal empire who brought 'tribute' to the court of the Son of Heaven, Yoshimitsu swallowed his pride and accepted from the Ming the title of 'King of Japan'. Yoshimitsu thereby restored a situation that the Chinese reckoned to have existed first during the Han dynasty until being grievously sundered by acts of piracy and war. The benefit to Yoshimitsu and to Japan was trade, which was henceforth to be carried on under the tally system that legitimated voyages and made piracy unnecessary.

The new licensed trade agreements with the Ming provided the stability that both governments needed to deal with piracy. In a dramatic incident in 1419 a large *wako* fleet was ambushed off Liaodong and perhaps a thousand Japanese pirates were relieved of their heads. At the same time other diplomatic discussions took place with the Korean court about ways to curb the *wako* who were still raiding that country. One result was a report from the Korean ambassador Pak So-saeng in 1429 recommending a direct approach to the individual *daimyo* who owned the territories where the pirates lurked. After all, as another ambassador reported in a curiously generous memorandum in 1444, these people lived in a barren land that constantly threatened them with starvation, so piracy was only natural to them.

THE PIRATE KINGS

As a result of these diplomatic efforts, piratical activities against Korea and China diminished greatly, but the *wako* were not to be left unemployed for long. Following the tragic Onin War in 1467, the centralised authority of the shogun virtually collapsed, leaving the field open for the numerous conflicts that we know as the Period of Warring States. In a similar process to the methods whereby landlocked *daimyo* established their territories by the thoroughly respectable business of stealing land and building castles on it, the more astute seafarers of Kyûshû and the Inland Sea entered the new Japanese aristocracy through the means of naval warfare. It was piracy by another name, and for the first time in centuries the *wako* were playing at home.

Just as in the days of the Taira in the 12th century, the numerous islands and inlets of the Inland Sea provided excellent pirates' lairs for their 16th-century equivalents. The most famous family name associated with the 'pirate kings' (such an expression for a sea-going *daimyo* is too good to be missed!) was Murakami. There were three active branches based on the islands of Noshima, Kurushima and Innoshima. The latter island now houses a very entertaining Pirates Museum. It is located next to the Konrenji temple where the members of the Murakami family lie buried. Among the exhibits on display is a hanging scroll with a portrait of Murakami Yoshimitsu, the greatest son of the Innoshima branch.

The museum also houses the helmet of Murakami Takeyoshi (1533–1604). As befits a sea dog, it bears a crest of a golden shell. Takeyoshi ruled from his castle located on the island of Noshima on one of the busiest and narrowest straits of Japan's Inland Sea. 'The people of the shores and sea coasts of other provinces each year pay him tribute for fear of being destroyed,' wrote one chronicler. The independence enjoyed by the pirate kings resembled in all particulars the lives of the provincial *daimyo* elsewhere in Japan who lived by war to defend their territories and to increase them. Certain customs had their own local flavour. For example, when the Murakami went into battle, the customary farewell meal included octopus, because with its eight arms it was protected against enemies from all directions.

By the mid-16th century the fragmentary nature of Japanese society meant that the *wako* of Kyûshû could turn their attentions towards China once again. Four hundred and sixty seven incidents of piracy in Chinese waters were recorded for the 1550s alone, and slaves once again formed part of the booty. On two occasions the tomb of the founder of the Ming dynasty narrowly escaped destruction at the hands of *wako*, but there was an important difference from earlier days. There were

Murakami Yoshimitsu was the leading 'pirate king' from the branch of the Murakami family based on the island of Innoshima in the Inland Sea. This hanging scroll of him is in the Pirates' Museum on Innoshima.

now as many Chinese pirates involved in the raids as there were Japanese. *Wako* was still the name used for the brigands, but the majority of them were no longer just Japanese but a mixed bag of Chinese renegades, Portuguese freebooters and other nationalities in one big happy family. The Chinese pirate Wang Zhi, who was beheaded in 1551, even had the audacity to make his headquarters on the Japanese island of Hirado.

RIGHT The 'pirate king' Murakami Takeyoshi (1533–1604) ruled from his castle located on the island of Noshima on one of the busiest and narrowest straits of Japan's Inland Sea. This waxwork of him is in the Pirates' Museum on Innoshima. His helmet bears a crest of a golden shell, as befits a sea dog. His banner proclaims the name of Hachiman, the *kami* of war.

OPPOSITE PAGE A model of a pirate ship of the Murakami family in the Pirates' Museum on Innoshima. It is of the *ataka bune* type, with a normal complement of 80 oarsmen and 60 fighting men. The sides are lowered for boarding, and the Murakami *mon* (badge) appears on the sail.

Otomo Sôrin was one *daimyo* who had to take some responsibility for the *wako*, if only because his conquests of Buzen and Chikuzen provinces placed several pirate lairs under his jurisdiction. In 1551, as a Chinese chronicle tells us:

Governor-general Yang Yi of the Ming dispatched Zheng Shungong who proceeded to Hirado in Hizen. He was able to meet with Otomo Yoshishige, and reprovingly said, 'We have had friendly ties for many years. Why are your people now causing havoc to our shores and taking our people prisoner? Stop behaving in this manner at once.'

Sôrin's reply was not entirely helpful. He pointed out that the need to protect his domains against neighbours made it very difficult to delegate troops to clear out the pirates. Besides, the piracy, he stated, was 'only the work of bandits on islands'.

As for Korea, by the end of the 15th century, commercial relations with Japan had moved on from piracy to the establishment of three licensed Japanese trading enclaves on the southern Korean coast. But so economically aggressive were the Japanese merchants that Korea tried to expel them, and in 1510 a major riot developed. The Sô *daimyo* of Tsushima was asked to control them, but responded instead by attacking Koje island himself in an echo of the *wako* raids of old. A new wave of piratical activity directed against Korea started in 1555 when a massive raid was launched against the coast of Chollado by 70 ships from the Gotô islands and Hizen. This action, the last of the large-scale *wako* incursions, proved to be almost a dress rehearsal for the Japanese invasion of Korea in 1592. Korean resistance all but collapsed. Left waiting for their commander to arrive from Seoul, the Korean troops gave in as the Japanese advanced, and by the time the general arrived he had no army to lead, only runaway soldiers hiding in the forests and no one left in reserve. On the Japanese side there was a more ironic precedent, because the sons of these same pirate kings would be back in Korean waters in less than half a century, pirates no longer, but transformed into the loyal and legitimate navies of the Japanese *daimyo*. They would provide the transport, the warships and some of the fiercest fighters for the greatest *wako* raid of all: Hideyoshi's invasion of Korea.

FROM PIRATES TO SEA LORDS

Experienced sailors such as Murakami Takeyoshi provided a vital contribution to samurai warfare during the Period of Warring States, and it was only the most completely landlocked *daimyo* who felt that he could dispense with a navy. The Hôjô, who had direct access to the Pacific Ocean, are known to have fought naval battles against the Satomi family. Even Takeda Shingen, whose lands encompassed the central mountain region of Japan, maintained his own inland navy on Lake Suwa. By 1569 the Takeda lands had expanded to give them a coastline captured from the former Imagawa territories on the Pacific coast, and five ships became the core of a new Takeda navy under the former Imagawa retainer Tsuchiya Sadatsuna. The fleet grew quickly as a response to the threat from the neighbouring Hôjô, and by 1575, when Tsuchiya Sadatsuna was killed at Nagashino, there were 50 large ships in the Takeda navy. They went into action against the Hôjô in 1580 near Omosu in Izu province. Takeda Katsuyori had set up his headquarters on land, from where he could watch his admirals launch an attack on the Hôjô ships. There was some fierce fighting before the ships disengaged, but even this demonstration of another dimension to the Takeda fighting capacity was not sufficient to save them from their ultimate collapse in 1582.

From 1560 onwards the most powerful *daimyo* in Japan was Oda Nobunaga, who defeated a series of rivals to control central Japan. The Môri, whose territories lay to the west, came into direct conflict with him when they began supporting his deadliest enemies, the Buddhist fanatics of the Ikkô-ikki. Their headquarters were the fortified cathedrals of Nagashima and Ishiyama Honganji, the latter being located where Osaka castle now stands. This gave the Ikkô-ikki a direct outlet to the Inland Sea, and the Môri kept them supplied by this route. The result was the first battle of Kizugawaguchi in 1578. There were few other naval battles during the Sengoku Period. The invasions of Shikoku and Kyûshû by Hideyoshi saw ships being used only for transport purposes, but the siege of the Hôjô castle of Shimoda in 1590 provides a unique example of a siege being conducted largely from the sea.

This is the Konrenji, the family temple of the Murakami family on the island of Innoshima. The old 'pirates' graveyard' is located among the trees immediately to the rear of the main building.

HIDEYOSHI, THE PIRATE-QUELLER

The unification of Japan achieved by Toyotomi Hideyoshi in 1591 inevitably took in the pirates. The process began in 1588 when Hideyoshi enacted the first of two ordinances that were to have a direct influence on the world of the warrior. This was the famous 'Sword Hunt', by which all weapons were to be confiscated from the peasantry and placed in the hands of the *daimyo* and their increasingly professional armies. By this act the means of making war were forcibly removed from anyone of whom Hideyoshi did not approve, because the Sword Hunt was much more than a search of farmers' premises. Minor *daimyo* whose loyalty was suspect, religious institutions that had the capacity for armed rebellion and recalcitrant village headmen were all purged in an operation that has parallels with Henry VIII's Dissolution of the Monasteries. The victims were told that the swords, spears and guns thus collected would not be wasted, but would be melted down to make nails for the enormous image of the Buddha that Hideyoshi was erecting in Kyôtô. The nation would therefore benefit from the operation in two ways. It would be spiritually blessed, and would be freed from the curses of war and rebellion which had caused such disruption and suffering in the past.

It is more than likely that the majority of the weapons seized were not actually destroyed but stored ready for future campaigns, but less well known was another edict issued on the same day as the Sword Hunt. It was aimed directly at the pirates. In their case the local representatives of the *daimyo* were not specifically looking for weapons but sought instead to obtain written oaths that no seafarer should engage in piracy. If any *daimyo* should fail to comply with the order and allow pirates to stay and practise their craft, then his fief would be confiscated. The Sword Hunts were followed by the Separation Edict of 1591, which formally divided the samurai class from the rest of society and did not explicitly mention seafarers, but its intentions towards them were no less clear for that. The peasants had been disarmed, and there was now to be a total separation between the military function and the productive (i.e. agricultural) function.

Hideyoshi's Sword Hunt, by which non-samurai were disarmed, played a large part in destroying the influence of the pirates in the remote areas of Japan. In this waxwork in the Date Masamune Historical Museum in Matsushima we see Date Masamune enforcing the Sword Hunt in his own territories.

Within a year of his reform of Japanese society, Hideyoshi launched the invasion of Korea. The main burden of supplying troops fell upon the *daimyo* whose lands were nearest to the peninsula, so the ex-*wako* of Kyûshû soon had the surprising duty of being commanded to carry out what amounted to a pirate raid with official government blessing. They responded with suitable loyalty, and attacked Korea with great ferocity. In a memorial to the Korean court, Admiral Yi Sun Sin wrote that 'the cruel Japanese are divided into two groups: one marching north through our heartland and another entering our coastal towns to perpetrate outrages.' There were no major battles in the latter operation, just the securing of land and sea communications using the weapon of terror, and it is perhaps for this reason that the Japanese movements are largely anonymous. In most cases it is impossible to identify the units engaged, and even the identity of the high-ranking Japanese commanders remains a mystery. No heroic chronicles record their movements in this war of rape, raiding and pillage which so resembled the *wako* depredations of yore, and it is only from the Korean records of the victories achieved against them that we know anything of their activities. A definite impression is given that these men, who were clearly not in the first rank of samurai heroes, were left very much to their own devices. The only prominent *daimyo* known to have taken part in the depredations were the Kurushima brothers and Kamei Korenori, all of whom had *wako* ancestors, but any other names are conveniently lost in the annals of samurai disgrace.

The story of how Admiral Yi defeated the Japanese navy using his famous armoured turtle ships is a familiar one that does not need retelling here. Suffice to say that the Japanese naval endeavours against Korea were almost a total disaster by the time the war ended in 1598. We also noted earlier how the survivors of the battle of Sekigahara in 1600 settled down under the Tokugawa in their fine new castles only to see many of them demolished on government orders. The development of trade overseas similarly came under Tokugawa control, and eventually brought to an end one other aspect of the sea-going samurai that we have not mentioned so far. This is the little-known topic of the samurai as overseas mercenaries.

SAMURAI OF FORTUNE

Mercenary warfare in its European meaning was virtually unknown in Japan itself. There were no Japanese *condottieri* (the notorious Italian mercenary captains), and no equivalent of the specialist weapons units for hire like the Genoese crossbowmen. The nearest parallel was the hiring of the famous ninja, in which Iga province had a valued speciality. Yet from the late 16th century onwards we find references to Japanese samurai fighting in foreign armies. In some cases there was an agreed contract. In others the mercenary-like activity sounds more like piracy by invitation.

One of the first foreign nations to employ Japanese mercenaries was Spain. Their mercenary activities included being signed up for a bizarre, yet perfectly serious attempt to conquer China for the Christian faith. The expedition was to be launched from the Philippines with up to 6,000 Japanese in the invading army of about 25,000 men. The scheme never got further than the planning stage because when it reached Madrid for approval in 1588 the Spanish had just had a little trouble with another Armada and were disinclined to approve other overseas ventures of that sort. The Spanish nevertheless employed a number of Japanese mercenaries when they invaded Cambodia in 1595. In spite of killing the king of Cambodia, the expedition was a failure, and the incursion was driven back down the Mekong river. In 1603 the Japanese distinguished themselves in the Philippines when they helped put down a Chinese rebellion against Spanish rule in Manila.

The distinction between merchants, mercenaries and pirates was often a fine one, and as Japanese overseas activities increased, the inhabitants of the coasts of Siam, Cambodia and Vietnam grew alarmed that a new generation of *wako* had appeared in the guise of mercenaries. In 1597 the Portuguese viceroy at Goa expressly forbade any Japanese from landing at Macao, and by 1605 the Spanish governor of the Philippines was expressing his fears about a possible Japanese invasion of the islands. He was particularly concerned about the large number of Japanese mercenaries in Spanish pay. The fear of the Japanese spread widely, and in December 1605 a certain John Davis became the first Englishman ever to be killed by a Japanese when his ship was involved in a fight with *wako*. His captain, Sir Edward Michelbourne, wrote afterwards:

About the 27th of December 1605 I met with a junk of the Japons, which had been pirating along the coast of China and Cambodia. Their pilots being dead, with ignorance and foul weather, they had cast away their ship on the shoals of the great island of Borneo, and to enter into the country of Borneo they durst not, for the Japons are not suffered to land in any port in India with weapons; being accounted a people so desperate and daring, that they are feared in all places where they come.

A year or so later a company of Japanese mercenaries serving the Portuguese in Malacca helped fight off an attempt to capture it by the Dutch admiral Cornelis Matelief de Jonge. The same admiral encountered a *wako* vessel some time later, and wrote that:

These Japanese were all brave men and looked like pirates, as indeed they were. They are a very determined race, for when they see they will be overwhelmed by the Chinese, they cut open their own bellies rather than fall alive into the hands of their enemies and be tortured to death.

Hideyoshi's invasions of Korea in 1592 and 1597 amounted to the largest ever pirate raids on Korea. This painting in the Namwon Memorial Museum shows the fall of the town of Namwon to Japanese troops in 1597. The gatehouse is burning, while rows of Japanese *ashigaru* fire their arquebuses.

As was the way of mercenaries the world over, other groups of Japanese were employed by the Dutch at about the same time. But the Dutch, like the Spanish before them, came to doubt the wisdom of employing them on a large scale, because 'they are lambs in their own country, but well-nigh devils outside of it.' In 1614 some Englishmen of the East India Company killed eight Japanese in a skirmish at Ayuthia, the Siamese capital, and in 1616 Richard Cocks' diary records an alarming incident reported to him from Ayuthia. An English trader called Mr Pitts had an argument with a certain James Peterson, and:

> went with three Japanese to bind him and take him prisoner. But Peterson laid so about him that he killed two of the Japanese, and made Pitts and the other run away. This Peterson is in great favour with the King of Siam, and therefore I marvel Mr Pitts would take this course, but Mr Mathias says it was done in drink.

The aggressive behaviour of Japanese merchants in rebellious Cambodia in 1623 caused friction with Siam (Thailand), so the king of Siam wrote to Shogun Tokugawa Hidetada to explain that Cambodia was a vassal state of Siam that needed to be punished. He added a dark warning that the Japanese in Cambodia should not try to intervene:

> My government intends therefore to take a convenient opportunity of raising forces by sea and land in order to overrun and subdue his territories. If the merchants of your honoured country who trade thither should be so misguided as to render him assistance when the war breaks out, they will run the risk of being hurt in the melee, which I fear will not be in accordance with the friendly feelings I entertain towards you.

Tokugawa Hidetada's reply was exactly what the king wished to read. These so-called 'merchants' were of no concern to the government of Japan. He wrote:

> If merchants of my country resident there should aid them to repel the attack of your honoured country, [and] you wish to exterminate

them, although it is not in accordance with the friendly relations
existing between Japan and Siam, this will, however, be perfectly
just, and you need not hesitate for a moment ... Merchants are fond
of gain and given up to greed, and abominable fellows of this kind
ought not to escape punishment.

It was a typical haughty samurai reaction to the unspeakable
activities of the mercantile classes, whoever they were.

THE KING AND YAMADA

The most important client country for samurai mercenaries was
Siam, where Japanese warriors provided a bodyguard for the
king and were highly valued in the role. A Dutchman called Van
Vliet wrote:

But the Japanese (numbering 70 to 80) are the best soldiers and
have always been highly esteemed by the various kings for their
bravery. The greater number of the soldiers are cowardly Siamese.

Another Dutchman, the head of the Dutch Factory (i.e.
trading post) at Ayuthia from 1628 until 1636, described the
Japanese mercenaries in the following words:

The best are some 500 or 600 Japanese soldiers, who are
wonderfully respected by the surrounding nationalities on account
of their reputation for manly valour, and are honoured and
respected by the Siamese kings.

The earliest reference to Japanese fighting for Siam occurs in
1579 in a Siamese source, but this is unfortunately not confirmed
by any Japanese record. It refers to a company of 500 Japanese
mercenaries helping the Siamese against an invasion by Burma
and Laos. The men may have been taken to Siam by Portuguese
ships, but it is strange that no names or locations are known. King
Naresuen of Siam was very active in Asian politics during his reign,
which coincided with Hideyoshi's invasion of Korea in 1592, and
actually offered China the use of the Siamese navy to fight the
Japanese fleet, a gesture that was politely declined.

It is not until 1606 that we find written records of intercourse between Japan and Siam. Tokugawa Ieyasu had been assured by his military advisors that Siamese gunpowder was of very good quality, so this became an important trading commodity. Japanese swords were equally valued in Siam, as were the men who wielded them. The most famous samurai ever to serve in this capacity was Yamada Nagamasa (1578–1633), whose romantic life has been embellished by legend. There is, however, a solid core of fact about Japan's great adventurer. He was born in Suruga province, and claimed to be a grandson of Oda Nobunaga. In 1615, when the political crisis made thoughts of foreign adventure a risky business, he sailed from Osaka in secret in a vessel bound for Formosa (Taiwan). After some time there he sailed for Siam, where his mercantile business prospered. At the time of a revolt against the king, Yamada gave him good advice, and soon found himself fighting as a mercenary for the king of Siam. In return for his loyal service he was given a Siamese princess as his wife and the governorship of a province.

The confidence he enjoyed from the king inevitably led to jealousy and accusations of power politics. Matters came to a head when the king became ill and entrusted much of the government to Yamada. A jealous minister turned the ailing king against the Japanese and arranged for Yamada Nagamasa to be poisoned as a preliminary to an attack on the Japanese settlement and the expulsion of its inhabitants. But the plot came to the ears of the Japanese, who took the initiative:

> They proposed therefore to proceed into the city with a small body of armed men, and as soon as the discharge of firearms was heard, every one who felt like a man would hurry to the city, and die there fighting, to the exaltation of the military renown of Japan. This proposal was received with enthusiasm, and the others swore they would all die together.

There was some bloodshed before the Japanese agreed to leave peacefully, but as the Japanese ships were departing they were attacked by Siamese ships. The Japanese drove them off

and successfully made their escape. The Siamese then called upon a Portuguese vessel that lay at anchor nearby. There was another skirmish, and the Japanese finally sailed away, counting 43 dead among their number.

But the Ayuthia affair was by no means over. Eight samurai had been absent on a pilgrimage to a Buddhist temple, and when they returned to the capital they were arrested and put in jail. They did not stay there for long, because news arrived that Siam was in peril. Word had reached Siam's enemies that the Japanese had been expelled. It says something for the reputation the Japanese enjoyed overseas that some 'Java people', a vague expression that may have meant Indonesian pirates, Dutch troops or even Portuguese, seized the opportunity to raid Siam. The king of Siam soon came to his senses, acknowledging that the Japanese 'belonged to a nation more feared by the Southerners than a fierce tiger'. He promised the captives their liberty if they would help rid his country of the invaders.

The eight Japanese acted with alacrity and proposed that as many Siamese troops as possible should be equipped with Japanese armour and helmets, the sight of which would terrify the attackers. Seventy suits of Japanese armour were found, and this number of Siamese was dressed up in them. Eight war elephants were also made available. The eight samurai took command of the disguised company together with an additional 500 Siamese soldiers, and placed a couple of small cannon on the back of each elephant. The army set out for the coast, and 'as soon as they came in sight of the Java ships, they began a furious cannonade, which would speedily have sunk the whole fleet, had they not prudently retreated'.

This bizarre incident was probably the last battle fought overseas by samurai mercenaries because, six years after Yamada Nagamasa's death, in 1639, the Tokugawa *bakufu* implemented Japan's Closed Country Edict. Although Japan was by no means as isolated from the rest of the world as is popularly believed, the restriction of trade to China and Korea meant that adventurers like Yamada Nagamasa had to find alternative outlets for their energies at home. Japanese naval enterprise was now carried out on a much smaller scale and, with the beginning of the

A gang of wako (Japanese pirates) disembark on the coast of Korea and begin a raid inland, 1380. (Artwork by Wayne Reynolds)

19th century, new ships were sighted in Japanese waters. They flew the flags of countries such as Russia and the United States, and promised that within a few years the world of the warrior, whether it was on dry land or the sea, would never be the same again.

CHAPTER EIGHT

The White Tigers

Aizu-Wakamatsu castle, seen here under snow, was the focus of the attack on the Aizu *han* by the armies of the new Meiji government.

Japan's seaborne isolation came to an end in July 1853 when four American warships entered the harbour of Uraga in Japan. They were commanded by Commodore Perry, who bore a letter from President Fillmore demanding that Japan sign a treaty of friendship with the United States. It was a defining moment in Japanese history. Fifteen years later the shogunate was abolished, the emperor was restored and Japan entered the modern world.

The enterprise is known to history as the Meiji Restoration, and presents a popular image of ex-samurai in top hats standing with their wives in crinolines to watch steam trains go by. But although it is customarily portrayed as a peaceful transition, the events that surrounded the Meiji Restoration saw conflicts as bitter as any that had erupted during the Period of Warring States. We noted earlier how Ii Naosuke's loyalty to the shogunate brought about his death. He was but one of many who fell victim to the passionate feelings that were held on both sides during this turbulent time. This chapter will describe many more, focusing on a little-known group of young samurai who also paid the ultimate price for their loyalty to the Tokugawa.

THE LOYAL *DAIMYO*

For the two and a half centuries prior to the Meiji Restoration Japan had existed under a system that successfully preserved the balance of power between the central government of the Tokugawa shoguns (the *bakufu*) and the localised government in the territories (the *han*) of the *daimyo*. All the internal affairs of a *han* were controlled from within the *han*, and the *daimyo* who ruled them fell into three categories. First were the four branches of the Tokugawa family who could supply an heir to the shogunate if the main branch became extinct. Then came the *fudai daimyo*, whose ancestors had already become the vassals of the Tokugawa prior to the battle of Sekigahara in 1600. They played a dual role. They ruled their own *han*, but also staffed the top positions in the *bakufu* hierarchy. The Ii family are a good example of the *fudai*. Last were the *tozama daimyo* who were descended from ancestors who had only sworn fealty to the Tokugawa after Sekigahara. Some had actually fought against the Tokugawa, and many had seen their lands confiscated or transferred during the Tokugawa Period. The house of Môri, at the extreme south-western tip of Japan's main island of Honshu, had been the second greatest feudal power in the country before Sekigahara, only to see its domains cut to the two provinces of Nagato and Suo. The *han* was known collectively as Chôshû. Even more remote was the Satsuma *han* in southern Kyûshû, the home of the once-glorious Shimazu family. Satsuma and Chôshû will come into our story both as supporters and enemies of the *bakufu*, but it is with one of the Tokugawa's most loyal supporters that we will be chiefly concerned. Aizu, in the north of Japan, gave as much as any other domain in its support of the shogun, and when the Restoration came, no other *han* lost so much or suffered as much for its devotion to a hopeless cause.

THE LORDS OF AIZU

The first *daimyo* of Aizu was Hoshina Masayuki, the half-brother of the third Tokugawa shogun, Iemitsu, who transferred him to Aizu-Wakamatsu castle in this mountainous, landlocked domain in 1643. Masayuki served the shogun with diligence and ruled his *han* in much the same way as did other *daimyo*. In 1699 their close relationship to the Tokugawa was given recognition when the family was permitted to use the family name of Matsudaira (Tokugawa Ieyasu's original family name) and to use the Tokugawa *mon* (badge). During the early 19th century,

The first *daimyo* of Aizu was Hoshina Masayuki, the half-brother of the third Tokugawa shogun, Iemitsu, who transferred him to Aizu-Wakamatsu castle in this mountainous, landlocked domain in 1643. Masayuki served the shogun with diligence.

when foreign ships were increasingly being seen off Japanese waters, the Aizu samurai shared in the task of providing coastal defences. In 1806, after Russian raids on settlements in Hokkaido, samurai from Aizu, most of whom had never been to sea before, patrolled the northern coast of the island.

The arrival of the US 'Black Ships' in 1853 was a traumatic incident for Tokugawa Japan. In this print we see the confusion caused as the Japanese army flying the Tokugawa flag marches down to confront the invaders.

When Commodore Perry made his fateful appearance in Japan Aizu was being ruled by a young *daimyo* called Matsudaira Katamori (1835–93). As he was only 17, he took no part in national politics, but these were dangerous times. In the year following the death of Ii Naosuke, the shogun's government trod carefully. Its members were sensitive to criticism, suspicious of the foreigner and fully aware of the threat posed by fanatical loyalists

who wanted nothing more than the shogun's disappearance from the scene. There were so many matters to decide. Should the country be opened up or not? Were the existing treaties fair to Japan? Could the foreign powers ever be resisted, given their evident military superiority? As to the last question, in 1861 Nagai Uta from the Chôshû *han* summarised the military situation in the following words:

If you suddenly begin an unplanned war, using samurai who have for several hundred years become accustomed to peace, even a three-year-old child can tell you what will happen.

Nagai's words referred specifically to the dangers inherent in Japan going to war with the United States, Great Britain, France or Russia. Civil conflict was another matter. As Ii Naosuke's assassination had shown, warfare could be conducted without the use of modern artillery and warships. The samurai sword still had a role to play in matters of internal power politics.

Matsudaira Katamori of Aizu finally stepped on to the stage of national politics in 1862 at the age of 27. He was made a *bakufu* advisor and a few months later he was appointed to the newly created post of Protector of Kyôtô. His duties required him to take control of the security of the emperor and palace and the policing of the city. Two of his senior counsellors in Aizu warned him against accepting the position, and compared the duties to that of trying to put out a fire while carrying firewood, but the demands of loyalty to the shogun that had sustained the Aizu domain for two centuries made him accept.

Policing Kyôtô proved to be no easy matter. Extremist samurai from the loyalist movement found their ranks swelled by other lawless elements as soon as the rule of law was perceived to be weakening. In early 1863 Hayashi Suke, a *bakufu* official, was murdered in his home in Kyôtô by a loyalist gang. Eight days later Ikeuchi Daigaku, a Confucian scholar, was killed and had his ears severed from his body. They were thrown into the courtyard of the residence of another intended victim with a note explaining that Ikeuchi had once been virtuous but had

When Commodore Perry made his fateful appearance in Japan, Aizu was being ruled by a young *daimyo* called Matsudaira Katamori (1835–93). He went on to serve the shogun with great loyalty until his domain was confiscated after the Boshin War. This waxwork at Matsushima is based on a contemporary photograph of him.

since joined the ranks of the evil pro-shogun officials. On other occasions the victim's hands, and from one his head, were used for the same purpose. In one more merciful incident the decapitation was limited to three wooden statues of the Ashikaga shoguns. They were put on display in Kyôtô with a placard that bore the words:

The traitors Ashikaga Takauji, Yoshiakira and Yoshimitsu. Today there exist traitors more villainous than these evil rebels ... If the evil practices existing since the time of Kamakura are not abolished ... the patriots of the country will rise up and avenge them.

THE FANATICS FROM CHÔSHÛ

The slogan of the loyalists was 'Sonno Joi' ('Revere the emperor and expel the barbarians'), and with the extremist faction now so dominant in Kyôtô, pressure was put on the shogun to set a definite date for the expulsion of the foreigners. The representatives from Chôshû were particularly insistent upon this point, and sent a letter to the court asking for a date to be fixed so that Chôshû could prepare for action. If the shogun would not expel the foreigners, then the emperor himself should lead his troops. Further vacillation by the shogun prompted a new round of terror.

The attitude being shown by Chôshû, who held the dominant position in Kyôtô, greatly alarmed other *han*. Many shared their views, but feared that Chôshû's belligerence would lead to disaster. Matsudaira Katamori of Aizu was a key figure in these deliberations, and in the autumn of 1863 joined the other influential *han* of Satsuma in carrying out a coup against Chôshû. Chôshû's influence at court was greatly curtailed following this incident, but back in Chôshû itself matters grew steadily worse. Foreign ships were fired on as they passed through the Shimonoseki strait, provoking a massive counter-bombardment from a joint fleet of Great Britain, France, Holland and the United States. Within a day the Chôshû forts had been demolished and their troops defeated by foreign landing parties. It seemed to the

The alliance between the two *han* of Satsuma and Chôshû was a defining moment in the years leading to the Meiji Restoration. It placed two of the most powerful armies in Japan against the shogun. This waxwork is in the Sakamoto Ryoma Historical Museum in Noichi, near Kochi. The figure on the left is Saigô Takamori.

shogun that the time had come to march against Chôshû, and by the end of 1864 150,000 samurai were poised at its borders, ready to attack. Matsudaira Katamori was originally chosen to lead the expedition, but it was felt that his role in Kyôtô was too important to be even temporarily abandoned. The expedition was no less successful for that, and returned from Chôshû with the severed heads of Chôshû's leaders.

THE MEIJI RESTORATION

If the *bakufu* thought they had solved the problem of Chôshû they were wrong, because a civil war within the *han* gave Chôshû new leaders who were even more radical than the ones who had formerly led the rebellion. Satsuma, too, felt aggrieved that it had not been given a voice in politics commensurate with its supportive role in 1863. Satsuma therefore withdrew from the Kyôtô coalition and entered into a secret pact with Chôshû. The restoration of the emperor was at last possible, so in January 1868 an alliance of Satsuma, Chôshû and other *han* seized the Kyôtô palace and proclaimed the return of imperial rule. As its first act, the new Meiji government stripped the shogun of his lands and abolished all *bakufu* offices.

The ever-loyal Matsudaira Katamori was one among many to be taken by surprise by this dramatic operation. Shogun Tokugawa Yoshinobu withdrew hurriedly to Osaka castle, and Katamori marched at the head of 1,600 Aizu troops in the shogun's army in an attempt to regain Kyôtô. During the four days of the battle of Toba-Fushimi, 120 Aizu samurai died and 158 were wounded. The shogun, accompanied by Matsudaira Katamori, fled by ship for Edo. Katamori urged that eastern Japan should unite in a war against the traitors to the shogun, but Tokugawa Yoshinobu was not for fighting. Instead he left Edo castle for a temple, where he waited to hear the decision of Japan's new rulers regarding his fate. Katamori retired to his domains in Aizu, protesting that he had shown no disloyalty to the emperor and had merely acted in self-defence against the act of aggression mounted by Satsuma and Chôshû.

THE AIZU CAMPAIGN

The new Meiji government could not ignore the sizeable core of pro-Tokugawa support that still existed in northern Japan, and first ordered the neighbouring Sendai *han* to attack Aizu. Sendai refused, so 3,000 government troops arrived in Matsushima Bay to put pressure on the *han's* rulers. But the heavy-handed treatment of Sendai backfired and provoked instead a loose alliance of northern *han* loyal to the shogun who were determined to resist the loyalist western domains that had staged the coup.

Government armies marched north, and by the spring of 1868 they had taken Edo. By early summer they were advancing to the north-east. Their strategy was to pick off the northern domains one by one. Their opponents fought bravely, but most surrendered quickly against the better armed and better organised government troops. The Meiji government originally planned to leave Aizu to the last, but their general Itagaki Taisuke pressed for an immediate attack before the snow started to fall. Soldiers from the warm climes of Satsuma would not fare well in the northern Japanese winter. He added, 'Aizu is the trunk and Sendai and Yonezawa are merely the branches and the leaves. Once the trunk is destroyed the branches and leaves will wither away.'

The events of the bitter Aizu campaign provide some of the saddest chapters in the history of the Boshin War, as the war of 1868 was to become known. Among other records of the operation there exists a remarkable account written by a man called Shiba Goro. At the time of the attack on Aizu-Wakamatsu castle he was only ten years old and so was sent away from the fighting. He later wrote his memoirs, and included details about the battles and the sad fate of his family. He tells us first about the call to arms issued by Matsudaira Katamori as the government forces advanced:

Even the children were enraged. I remember venting my anger by whacking my wooden sword against trees and bushes. 'Take that, you good-for-nothing potato samurai!' ... 'Potato samurai' was what we contemptuously called the Satsuma men, since we knew that the people of Satsuma, too poor to eat rice, lived on a diet of sweet potatoes.

Shiba Goro also describes watching his sisters practise with their wooden *naginata* (halberds) in the garden 'with white bands tied around their hair and kimono sleeves tucked up'. The rumours he was hearing about the war confirmed everyone's feeling that even women might have to fight:

... rumours circulated of troops running wild. According to one rumour, ronin from Satsuma and Choshu were setting fires and

murdering people in Edo and other places to stir up unrest, bringing further dishonour to the Tokugawa and foment hatred of Aizu. According to another rumour, the enemy troops left in their wake the corpses not only of soldiers, but also of innocent townsmen, peasants, women and children.

Shiba Goro then mentions the four battalions into which the Aizu army was organised. Most of Aizu's 7,000 troops, 3,000 of whom were peasant recruits, were fighting beyond the *han* borders. The four remaining units were named romantically after the god who was believed to guard one of the compass directions in the Chinese military classic, *The Art of War*. They were grandiose names for what was a pitifully small army, which consisted in total of 2,700 peasant recruits commanded by 380 samurai. The Seiryutai (blue dragon corps) were men aged between 36 and 49. They had responsibility for the defence of the *han* borders. The Shujakutai (red sparrow corps) were aged from 18 to 35 and constituted the main fighting force of the domain. The Genbutai (black warrior corps) were veterans of 50 and over who were charged with the defence of Aizu-Wakamatsu castle. Finally, there was the Byakottai (white tiger corps), youths aged 16 to 17 who were to constitute a reserve force.

The Blue Dragons were first to feel the impact of the government advance when Itagaki Taisuke decided to make a rapid strike against Aizu-Wakamatsu. Estimates of the number of his troops range from 10,000 to 30,000, so Aizu was heavily outnumbered. He started out on a road that led south-west from Nihonmatsu, his most recent gain. But this was a feint, because he then took a route across the Bonari Pass northwards and crossed into Aizu. Here he found the Aizu troops waiting for him. His soldiers soon drove them back and on 7 October seized a fortress at Inawashiro beside the lake of the same name. There was still a chance to halt their advance at the Nippashi river, which flowed out of Lake Inawashiro, so the men of Aizu took up positions at the strategic Jurokkyo bridge. But once again they were driven back to the open ground known as Tonoguchihara.

ABOVE Like the samurai of old, whose retainers held back the enemy to provide a moment of quiet, the 20 White Tigers, of whom 11 were 17 years old and nine were only 16, commit *hara kiri*. They had sufficient time to perform the act in classic samurai style, their grandstand view of the collapse of Aizu's hopes adding further drama to the scene.

RIGHT The statue commemorating the White Tigers that stands outside Aizu-Wakamatsu station. Although all the families of Aizu were exiled, the present inhabitants celebrate their memory with great reverence.

THE DEATH OF THE WHITE TIGERS

It is at this point that the young White Tigers come into the story. Early in the afternoon of 7 October they ceremonially marched past their *daimyo* Matsudaira Katamori at his headquarters located to the north-east of the city beside Mount Iimori. They set off for Tonoguchihara amid wind and rain and took up positions in the early evening. Gunfire could clearly be heard as they prepared their evening meal. For many of them it was the last food they would ever eat. The following morning a deep morning mist first obscured their view, and as it cleared hundreds of government troops, supported by artillery, could be seen moving across the plain

towards the position where the White Tigers had concealed themselves among bushes. The young warriors discharged small-arms fire, but as the government troops began to spread out they realised they were heavily outnumbered and ordered a retreat.

In the confusion of the withdrawal one group of White Tigers under the immediate command of Shinoda Gisaburo became detached from their comrades. Some of them were wounded, but as they were familiar with the surrounding countryside they managed to make a successful escape from the pursuing enemy by scrambling through an irrigation tunnel. It led through the edge of Iimoriyama to the precincts of the Itsukushima Shrine. Here, at least, they were safe from their pursuers until they had regained sufficient strength to move on to join in the defence of Aizu-Wakamatsu castle.

The castle could be seen in the distance from their vantage point on the slopes of Iimoriyama, but as they gazed at it they could see smoke arising from its keep. The castle had fallen. The cause of Aizu and its support for the shogun was hopelessly lost, so what course of action was open to loyal samurai other than to commit suicide within sight of the blazing castle? And that is precisely what they did. Like the samurai of old whose retainers held back the enemy to provide a moment of quiet, the 20 White Tigers, of whom 11 were 17 years old and nine were only 16, committed *seppuku*. They had sufficient time to perform the act in classic samurai style, their grandstand view of the collapse of Aizu's hopes adding further drama to a scene that would not have disgraced the mass immolation of the Hôjô at Kamakura in 1333. Some wrote farewell poems. Some acted as seconds for their friends. All used their daggers, and soon all but one of them lay dead. The survivor, Iinuma Sadakichi, had performed *seppuku* and was later found unconscious but alive.

THE DESTRUCTION OF AIZU

The great tragedy of the suicide of the White Tigers, if the loss of 19 young lives was not enough, was that, just as in the case of Yamamoto Kansuke at the battle of Kawanakajima in 1561, their sacrifice had been based on an incorrect assumption. Aizu-Wakamatsu castle had not fallen. Their deaths had therefore been unnecessary, and deprived the garrison of a service that might have helped prevent the almost inevitable capture that happened soon afterwards. Instead, within two days of starting out from Nihonmatsu, Itagaki Taisuke's government army was in possession of a gate in the northern outer wall of the castle. At this point the Aizu leaders rang the fire bell, which was the agreed signal for the elderly men, women and children to seek safety in the castle. They had, however, been advised by Matsudaira Katamori that although it was his intention to 'fight to the death to wipe out the stain on Aizu's honour', the non-combatants were free to act as they wished. The decisions that many of them took put them into the same category as the White Tigers. One samurai's 14-year-old son, wrote afterwards:

I hastened to the inner enclosure of the castle. I knew of course I would never return home ... not that I had the time to think of such matters ... All the women in my family had resolved to die, and yet, as I took leave, not one person shed a tear.

Many of the non-combatants stayed at home simply because they felt that their presence within the castle would hinder the fighting men and needlessly consume vital food supplies. This was a particularly brave decision in view of the rumours of Satsuma and Chôshû samurai slaughtering civilians in Edo. It may have been this fear of being killed, rather than the demands of samurai tradition, that led to the remarkable events that followed, because 230 non-combatants are known to have taken their own lives as Aizu-Wakamatsu fell. Young Shiba Goro, who was later to commit his feelings to paper, had been moved to a place of safety, but while he was away his grandmother, mother, oldest brother's wife and two sisters killed themselves. In the family of Saigô Tanomo, a senior retainer of the Aizu *han*, his mother, wife, five daughters and two sisters killed themselves. Other women in his extended family also committed suicide,

making a total of 22 female deaths from this one family. His sisters and daughters even composed farewell poems:

Each time I die and am reborn in the world
I wish to return as a stalwart warrior.

These were the words left behind by his older sister. The younger wrote:

I have heard that this is the way of the warrior
And so I set out on the journey to the land of the dead.

Other women accompanied their menfolk to the castle, where they assisted in the defence and were fully prepared to go into battle themselves. Shiba Goro writes about his conversation with a survivor:

According to Shiro, the women in the castle had played an extremely courageous part in the defence. Whenever a cannonball landed they ran to the spot and covered it with wet mats and rice sacks before it could explode. They cooked meals and nursed the wounded without respite, heedless of the damage done to their clothes. Bespattered with blood, they had outdone themselves in helping the men. And they had been fully prepared, if necessary, to change into their white kimono and charge into the enemy with their halberds.

Further confirmation of the bravery of the women of Aizu comes from an unusual source. Dr William Willis was a British doctor who accompanied the government troops during the Aizu campaign to help the wounded. On entering the town he treated several hundred of the Aizu wounded, whom he found 'in a deplorable state of filth and wretchedness', and in a memorandum dated 23 January 1869 Willis refers to the bravery and energy of the women in the castle:

They cut off their hair, busied themselves in preparing food, nursing the wounded, and in not a few instances, shouldered the rifle and bore a share in the fatigues of watching.

By the time the government troops had obtained their first toehold on the castle about 1,000 Aizu men had returned from duties elsewhere to strengthen the numbers inside the castle. The defence continued with night raids being launched on the government positions, until on 29 October Itagaki launched an all-out offensive. His troops burned the samurai houses in the outer castle precincts while 50 cannon pounded the castle day and night, some from as far as over a mile away. The Aizu troops responded with old-fashioned 4lb mortars with a range of only 85 yards (77m), but on 6 November, one month after the siege had begun, a white flag was raised above the northern gate. During the nine months between the battle of Toba-Fushimi that had seen the shogun driven out of Kyôtô and the fall of Aizu-Wakamatsu castle, 2,610 Aizu men had died in action.

As the above account shows, there was great bravery shown by all ages and from all social classes in the defence of the domain of Aizu. As far as Aizu was concerned, they themselves represented the real government of the shogun, nor were they any less loyal to the sacred person of the emperor because of it. But the Meiji rulers who defeated them took a different view. In a cruel act of retribution the entire *han* of Aizu was confiscated, and the following year the surviving samurai of Aizu were sent to detention camps. Matsudaira Katamori was sent to Tokyo under a sentence of death that was commuted to life-long house arrest. Afterwards, in a symbolic gesture of generosity, he was given the post of guard of the funeral temple of Tokugawa Ieyasu at Nikko. One of the domain elders was less fortunate, and in a bizarre echo of ancient samurai tradition was ordered to commit *seppuku*.

Some time around the beginning of 1870 the infant son of Matsudaira Katamori was given permission to revive the family name and line, but he was not restored to Aizu. Instead he was granted lands on the Shimokita Peninsula in what is now Aomori prefecture. It was barren land of volcanic ash

OVERLEAF The defenders of Aizu-Wakamatsu castle, as depicted in a woodblock print. The youth of the samurai is delicately represented.

buried for half the year in snow. The samurai detainees were allowed to leave their camps for their new homeland in the spring of 1870. They were not up to farming the inhospitable land, and many perished from malnutrition and disease. Local villagers who saw them eating wild plants and roots called them the 'Aizu caterpillars'.

The punishment inflicted upon Aizu surpassed in vindictiveness the treatment of any other 'rebels' during the time of the Meiji Restoration. No other opponents of the new order in Japan saw their lands confiscated, their samurai sent into detention and their people exiled. Nor did the people of Aizu ever forgive the leaders of Chôshû and Satsuma. They spoke of their enemies as the 'western army' – no one in Aizu could bear to call the Satsuma and Chôshû men 'government troops'.

The exile of the Aizu samurai was a sad end to such a late flowering of samurai heroism, but in Aizu-Wakamatsu today the resistance of 1868 is commemorated with pride and gusto. On leaving the railway station one is confronted by a bronze statue of the White Tigers, and this is but one of several memorials and museums within the city. Most exhibits concentrate on the gallant youths, but also take pride in the samurai spirit shown by the Aizu women. The memorial of the White Tigers centres on the mountainside of Iimoriyama, where one can see the spot where they committed *seppuku* and the nearby row of 19 identical graves.

Above the graveyard, however, is a chilling addition to the scene. During the 1930s Mussolini was told the story of the White Tigers, and presented the city of Aizu-Wakamatsu with a memorial in the form of a bronze eagle on top of a marble column. It bears the words in Italian, 'to the spirit of *bushido*'. To the Italian Fascists the White Tigers had illustrated the principles of ruthless self-sacrifice that within a decade would link Italy and Hitler's Germany to the modern manifestation of the samurai spirit. So the Fascist eagle looks down upon the samurai graves, its back turned to the distant view of Aizu-Wakamatsu castle, from where in 1868 the sight of black smoke led to one of the saddest and

During the 1930s, Mussolini was told the story of the White Tigers, and presented the city of Aizu-Wakamatsu with a memorial in the form of a bronze eagle on top of a marble column. It bears the words in Italian, 'to the spirit of *bushido*'. To the Italian Fascists the White Tigers had illustrated the principles of ruthless self-sacrifice that within a decade would link Italy and Hitler's Germany to the modern manifestation of the samurai spirit.

most unnecessary chapters in the bloody history of the world of the samurai.

The suicide of the White Tigers is nonetheless important as a symbol of samurai endeavour that links the medieval world to the modern. It is an event that expresses through deeds the words of the poet Basho, whose eulogy for the passing of the samurai was expressed in the following terms:

The murmuring of the summer grass
All that is left
Of the warriors' dream

There on the hillside of Iimori the grass blows in the wind to remind us of the darkest side of the world of the warrior.

CHAPTER NINE

Last of the samurai

Saigô Takamori is shown here in a hanging scroll that illustrates the size of the man, who was large in personality as well as physique.

Of the three *han*, Aizu, Chôshû and Satsuma, that were so deeply involved in the Meiji Restoration, the third, Satsuma, now demands our attention. We saw in the previous chapter how the reforms of the Meiji Restoration flew in the face of the tradition and isolationism of its founding fathers. The abolition of the samurai class was the most severe blow of all, and it is not surprising that the events of 1876 provoked a reaction from fanatics among the ranks of former samurai. Several insurrections and outrages occurred elsewhere in Japan during that momentous year, but all were put down quickly and efficiently by Japan's new conscript army. Then, early in 1877, a further rising happened. It was a samurai revolt on a scale much larger and more serious than any that had preceded it. It was led by Japan's most famous general, and it originated from Japan's most formidable samurai clan. It is known in Japanese history as the 'Seinan' War, a title which simply means the war 'in the south-west'. To English-speaking historians it is remembered as the Satsuma Rebellion.

To understand the origins of the Satsuma Rebellion it is necessary to backtrack somewhat to describe what had happened to Satsuma in the years following the Meiji Restoration. Frustrated by the western-style reformers, Saigô Takamori, one of the great leaders of the Meiji Restoration, had withdrawn from the government in October 1873 and retired to his native Satsuma. There he had busied himself setting up a series of organisations that bore the somewhat euphemistic title of 'Private Schools'. The curriculum of these institutions, of which 120 were established in the province, revealed that they were effectively military academies to train a Satsuma-led private army. Candidates seeking admission to these schools were required to swear to an oath that they would be faithful unto death, and then seal it with their own blood. Not surprisingly, the Meiji government in Tokyo became alarmed by these developments. Also, as the Satsuma clan had been instrumental in establishing the Meiji regime in the first place, a large quantity of arms and ammunition was located in Kagoshima. This had, of course, been officially imperial property since 1871 but, with the growth of the Private Schools, the Tokyo authorities decided to transfer the entire contents of the Kagoshima arsenal to Osaka, where they could more easily keep an eye on it. In a secret night operation on 30 January 1877 a ship was sent to collect the equipment. Their arrival was discovered, and the ship's crew found themselves attacked by more than a thousand Satsuma warriors. The government officials fled empty-handed, and the Satsuma samurai seized the imperial arsenal for their own.

Saigô Takamori had been absent from Kagoshima on a hunting trip when the incident happened, but had returned immediately to find the province in turmoil, with rumours circulating about a government conspiracy to have him assassinated. Fears of direct military intervention from Tokyo were also expressed. In the background, of course, were the burning issues of samurai swords and samurai pensions, so on 13 February 1877, the Satsuma soldiers from the Private Schools were organised into tactical units. Satsuma now had its own army in reality. A European correspondent wrote:

Saigô's men were but partly armed with rifles. Most of them were equipped with the keen double-handed swords of feudal times and with daggers and spears. It seemed to be their opinion that patrician samurai could rush into close quarters with the heimin (common people) and easily rout them – granting even that they were armed with rifles and bayonets. And it was reported that the astute Saigô ordered his soldiers not to kill the poor plebs in the government ranks, but rather to slash them well about the legs so

*as to disable them and render it necessary for each man thus
wounded to be borne off the field by two able-bodied comrades –
thus depriving the opposing ranks of three soldiers instead of one.*

This passage is undoubtedly a romantic exaggeration. Saigô
Takamori was not such an extreme conservative as to believe
that samurai swords and bravery were all that a modern army
needed. The sword was indeed the universal weapon, but in
addition they carried Snider and Enfield rifles, some carbines
and pistols, and enough ammunition for about 100 rounds per
man. The training in the Private Schools had also included
artillery and engineering techniques from the West.

SAIGÔ TAKAMORI GOES TO WAR

On 15 February 1877, under deep snow, Saigiô's advance guard
left Kagoshima for the north. Romantic spirits among the
samurai saw symbolic significance in the snow, for it had been
on a snowy night that the famous 'Forty-Seven Rônin' had
carried out their celebrated deed of vengeance. There was also a
poignant echo from Japanese history as Saigô Takamori bade
farewell to his 12-year-old son in the way of the hero Kusunoki
Masashige. With such analogies ringing in their ears, the
Satsuma army headed for their first objective – Kumamoto castle.

Kumamoto was the castle into which Katô Kiyomasa had
poured all the experience he had gained during the Korean War.
When the Meiji government had taken over responsibility
for the army from the individual *daimyo*, they had established
area commands throughout Japan. The command for Kyûshû
was based at Kumamoto, confirming the importance that Katô
Kiyomasa had originally envisaged for it. The castle was also
the only major obstacle in the way of Saigô Takamori marching
his men through Kyûshû and on eventually to Tokyo. Beyond
Kumamoto was the road to the strategic port of Nagasaki, which
would provide Saigo with sea transport and help him secure a
hold over the whole of Kyûshû.

Saigô Takamori expected either that the Kumamoto garrison
would let him pass unhindered, or that overcoming them would
be an easy matter. He knew that in the garrison were many

survivors of a bizarre suicide raid by fanatical samurai the year before. The group had called themselves 'the League of the Divine Wind', in other words *kamikaze*. In the words of a Western commentator, their army of 170 men 'dressed in beetle-headed helmets and old armour made of steel and paper laced with silk, and armed with spears and swords', carried out a night raid on the castle. More than 300 imperial troops were massacred in their beds by samurai swords. The insurgents then retired to the hills, and finding that there was no likelihood of a general uprising to support them, 84 of their number committed *seppuku*. The rest fought the imperial troops who had pursued them, and either surrendered or were killed.

With this recent precedent in mind the vanguard of the Satsuma army reached Kawashiri, a short distance south of Kumamoto, on 19 February, having covered the 106 miles from Kagoshima in four days despite heavy snow and intense cold. As their way was blocked by troops of the imperial army, the Satsuma men halted and, when Saigô's main body arrived on 21 February, a headquarters base was established. Meanwhile the Tokyo government had not been idle. Ships were steaming towards Hakata and Nagasaki with reinforcements.

The first shots of the Satsuma Rebellion were fired at 1.15 pm on 21 February when the troops of the Kumamoto garrison who had blocked Saigô's advance at Kawashiri opened fire on the rebels. The imperial troops were quickly overcome and withdrew into the shelter of Kumamoto. Outside its walls now sat Saigo Takamori with a Satsuma army that was three times larger than the imperial garrison. One of Saigô's subordinates, who had once himself been in command at Kumamoto, advocated an all-out assault. Saigô's decision was for a more planned approach, with a frontal attack from the south-east by 2,500 troops and a rear attack by 3,000 from the north-west, holding back 3,400 men in reserve. All other troops were occupied with reconnoitring the movements of any other imperial troops that may be approaching.

THE SIEGE OF KUMAMOTO

Leading the garrison of Kumamoto was General Tani Tateki. In the romantic legends that surround the image of Saigô Takamori

This statue of General Tani stands in the grounds of Kumamoto castle, the government possession that he heroically defended against the attacks led by Saigo Takamori's rebels.

as 'the last of the samurai' there is little space for a regular, Westernised soldier. But brave Tani deserves more recognition that he customarily receives. Under his command were 2,000 men from the 13th Infantry Regiment with about 1,800 soldiers from the 14th Infantry Regiment based normally at Kokura at the extreme northern tip of Kyushu. This made the garrison up to about 3,800 men. A besieged general, cut off from all contact with his headquarters, is a lonely figure. General Tani knew that the fate of Japan depended on him holding Kumamoto against Saigô until the full imperial army could throw its strength against him. But how best would he do this? He could sit tight within the castle, or take the fight outside the walls and do battle. A lack of

The massive stone bases and walls of Kumamoto castle bear testimony to Katô Kiyomasa who designed them early in the 17th century, and to General Tani, who defended them late in the 19th century.

information about his enemy made a decision difficult, and there was also the question of the morale of the Kumamoto garrison. The humiliating tragedy of the suicide attack the previous year had left them badly shaken. Moreover, many of Tani's officers were themselves natives of Satsuma. If even their loyalty was questionable, what was there to conclude about the loyalty of the 40,000 inhabitants of Kumamoto, who faced seeing their homes destroyed as the area became a civil war battlefield?

This is not to say that General Tani was not prepared. From the time that the first reports had reached him of Saigo's intentions, he had secretly augmented the castle's defences with ammunition dumps, bamboo fences and landmines. At the same time, he made a grand show of carrying out memorial services for the men killed during the suicide attack, hoping thereby to identify the interests of the local people with that of the imperial garrison.

It was at that point that fate played a strange part in the unfolding drama. On the morning of 19 February, as the rebels approached the castle, a fire broke out in a large storehouse and quickly spread, destroying nearly all of the castle's food supply. At first Tani's worst fears appeared to be confirmed as panic and indiscipline prevented the control of the fire. But soon the officers restored order, and many acts of individual heroism occurred. Then a far more serious situation developed, because the burning storehouse overlooked one of the interior castle walls, and at the bottom of its curving slope lay the castle's entire stock of reserve ammunition. Regardless of the danger, the garrison began removing the ammunition to a safe place, but no sooner had they begun when the storehouse collapsed. It fortunately fell inwards and away from the explosives, so not only was the precious ammunition saved, but the shared danger forged a bond between officers and men that had not previously existed, and the defenders of Kumamoto began to gel as one. Over the next few days a furious attempt was made to buy up all the available food from Kumamoto city, and it was on 20 February that a welcome reinforcement of 600 police troops arrived. Now confident of local support, Tani reluctantly ordered the destruction of several hundred local houses to provide a clear field of fire. The sluices were opened to let the moats fill with water, and Kumamoto waited, ready for the rebel assault, like 'fish in a kettle'.

SUICIDE SQUADS

Saigô's first move against Kumamoto was heralded by the rather quaint action of firing 'arrow letters' into the castle calling upon the defenders to surrender. The text included the following words: 'As we feel pity for those who have been compelled to remain in the castle against their will, we will pardon them if they at once throw down their arms and submit to us.' The exhortations produced no response, and in the early hours of 22 February the advance guard of the Satsuma army began their assault on Kumamoto castle from the south-east. As the hours went by the attack spread round the outer walls and small-arms fire could be heard coming from all directions. For the next two days, furious attacks were carried out on the castle ramparts. The Satsuma samurai, their ancestral swords in hand, clambered up the walls like suicide squads to be shot down by the rifle fire

In this print of the Satsuma Rebellion we see Saigô Takamori's rebels fighting against government troops.

from Tani's conscript army. Many were the hand-to-hand combats that happened on the black walls of Kumamoto as fanaticism met determination, and an old loyalty was pitted against a new version of samurai honour. But Tani's men held firm, and no foothold was gained by 24 February, at which point Saigô regrouped and withdrew 2,000 out of his original attacking force of 5,000 to move north to await the imperial reinforcements that he knew would be on their way.

The siege then developed into a war of attrition, with casualties mounting on both sides of Kumamoto's walls. Saigô was now forced to fight on three fronts, against the castle, against the imperialists in the south, and soon against a huge reinforcement that moved down from the north. This the rebels managed to do against all the odds. To add to the infantry attacks along the walls, Saigô established artillery positions on the hills around the castle from which a bombardment began, while from within the garrison brave attempts were made to contact units outside. Two civilian messengers were the first to try and run Saigô's gauntlet, but they were apprehended. The garrison of Kumamoto learned of their fate only when the men's severed heads were tossed back into the castle the following morning. Two days later, however,

The keep of Kumamoto castle was the focus for the main action of the Satsuma Rebellion. It held out against attacks from modern cannon and from waves of sword-wielding samurai.

Shishido Masateru, a former superintendent of the castle, disguised himself as a carpenter and managed to slip through the siege lines to contact the imperial army. In an echo of the famous tale of Torii Sune'emon at the siege of Nagashino in 1575, his safe return with the news that relief was on its way greatly encouraged everyone within. General Tani and Shisido are the only two people ever to have had their lives commemorated with a statue inside Kumamoto castle. Their statues still stand today.

By 1 March an inventory indicated that the castle had probably only 19 days of rations left, and ammunition was now so limited that the defenders had begun the highly dangerous business of digging up unexploded Satsuma shells and firing them back at the besiegers. As the siege progressed the Satsuma lines moved ever nearer to the castle walls, and at one point got so close that the opponents were able to exchange banter with one another. As is so often the case in a civil war, fathers encountered sons, and brother met with brother fighting on the other side. Sometimes news was passed on. At other times, bullets flew and heads rolled from sharp samurai swords. Day by day, food supplies grew less. The supply of fresh vegetables was soon exhausted, meals of rice and barley were restricted to two per day for combatants, while non-combatants received only gruel. The interior moats were drained to a minimum to make it easier to catch the fish within them, in spite of the obvious advantage it gave to the enemy. The killing of a horse was a cause for rejoicing as the dead animal was immediately cooked and eaten. The garrison's frugality paid off, because a further inventory of stores showed that they now had theoretically a longer supply of food than when previously estimated.

On 7 April it was decided that Major Oku Yasukata would lead a detachment out of the castle to link up with the imperial troops known to be in the south near Kawashiri. The sally was almost an act of desperation, and was accompanied by the feeling than even if the men were killed then it would mean less mouths to feed. In fact the operation was a success, and the unit either passed the Satsuma sentries by or killed them with their silent swords. On being attacked by the rebels, Oku managed to seize some supplies and held the road to Kumamoto open long enough for the garrison to be enriched by the addition of a hundred rifles, 3,000 rounds of ammunition and several hundred bags of rice. When the Satsuma army finally cut the road, Oku broke through again and joined up with the imperialists in Kawashiri.

By mid-April, the pressure from the imperial army was beginning to tell, but Saigô's excellent generalship prevented them from relieving the castle. Meanwhile the advance from the south continued like the sweep from the hand of a clock. The orders were to stand firm as soon as they had secured positions on the north bank of the Midori river. Kumamoto might not have been relieved for some time had it not been for a certain Lieutenant-Colonel Yamakawa, whose subsequent conduct reminded the rest of the imperial army that the spirit of the samurai was not quite dead among the imperial troops. Instead of halting, he continued his advance, and at about 4.00 pm he appeared in front of the castle gate to relieve the castle on his own. An imperial soldier stood at the gates of Kumamoto. All firing had ceased, and pausing for a moment to identify the new arrivals, those in the garrison soon realised that the ordeal was now over.

AFTERMATH

The relief of Kumamoto castle was the turning point in the Satsuma Rebellion. The imperial troops now had little to fear from Saigô's army. Between April and September 1877, the course of the action dwindled to a series of pursuits and dispersals across southern Kyûshû. Once the siege of Kumamoto had ended, the government troops concentrated their efforts on taking Kagoshima, which Saigô had been forced to leave poorly defended. Even though many of Saigô's men were defeated at other engagements, he, together with a now pitifully small number of followers, managed to break through the imperialist cordon and entered Kagoshima.

Together with only a few hundred men Saigô took up a position on Shiroyama, the site of the former castle of the mighty Shimazu at the centre of the city. Thirty thousand government troops slowly closed in on him. By all accounts Saigô Takamori had already made up his mind either to be killed in battle or to die at his own hand. The night before the final assault he behaved like the samurai of old, listening to the music of the Satsuma lute, performing an ancient sword dance, and composing poetry:

> If I were a drop of dew
> I could take shelter on a leaftip
> But, being a man
> I have no place in this whole world.

He then exchanged cups of *sake* with his chief officers, and prepared for the attack by the government forces that began at four o'clock the following morning. Saigô and his followers

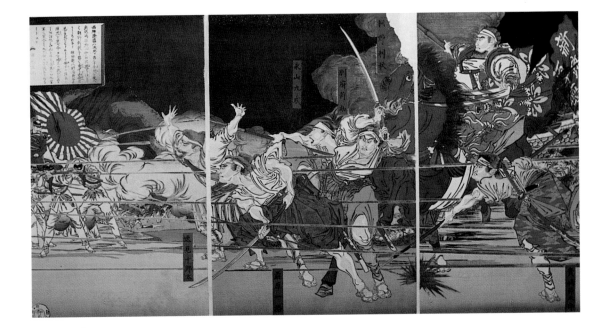

The last act of the Satsuma Rebellion was Saigô Takamori's defiant final battle on the slopes of Shiroyama in Kagoshima, shown here in a dramatic print.

moved down the hill under intense enemy fire. Soon he was hit in the groin by a bullet and could no longer walk. His follower Beppu Shinsuke lifted him up and carried him down the mountain until they came to a place that Saigô regarded as suitable for *seppuku*. It was the gate of a former mansion of the Shimazu. Saigo bowed in the direction of the imperial palace and then cut himself open. Beppu Shinuske acted as his second, and as soon as Saigo's head was safely disposed of he charged down the hill and was mown down by gunfire.

The Satsuma Rebellion was the last organised attempt until the 1930s to oppose the government by force. It was also the final war of the samurai. With the passing of Saigô Takamori died the final act of organised military resistance to the reforms of the Meiji government. Japan's last samurai army had been pitted against a force of conscripted farmers, and had failed. The human cost of the lesson was enormous. More than 60,000 imperial troops fought in the Satsuma Rebellion and suffered 7,000 deaths and 9,000 wounded. Of the total rebel strength of 30,000 only a handful survived. The symbolic effect of the defeat was every bit as dramatic. The Western correspondent quoted above had watched the imperial force leave Tokyo, and had written:

The garden of the Sengan-En, the mansion of the Shimazu *daimyo* of Satsuma, showing the island volcano of Sakurajima out in Kagoshima Bay.

Someone said that the heimin, or common people, comprising a large part of the imperial forces, would never be able to face the samurai of Satsuma – that one samurai would put five heimin to flight, and as the troops marched through Tokyo on their way south they were the recipients of pitying comments that they were but so much meat for Saigô's swords.

That such comments were proved wrong was the death blow for the samurai class. The belief that only samurai could fight had been finally and dramatically laid to rest around the walls of Kumamoto castle, and the death of Saigô at Shiroyama was but the confirmation of it. As for Kumamoto castle, although much of it was destroyed in the fighting, the ghost of Katô Kiyomasa could have looked down upon the scene with much satisfaction. Modern artillery, possessing a power he could only have dreamed of , had failed to shatter the huge stone foundations on which it lay. His wells had ensured that the garrison never suffered from thirst, and his walls proved a fine defence against the swinging sword blades with which Kiyomasa would have

This statue of Saigô Takamori stands at the foot of Shiroyama in Kagoshima, where he committed suicide as his rebellion finally collapsed. Saigô Takamori may justly be regarded as the last of the samurai.

The armaments of new Japan, illustrated in this print from the time of the Russo-Japanese War.

been so familiar. Katô Kiyomasa's dream of an impregnable castle had been tested and proved against an enemy that he would have recognised and understood. They may have carried rifles in addition to their swords and used modern cannon, but Kumamoto had withstood the final siege of a Japanese castle by an army that was predominantly driven by the ideals and technology of the world of the samurai.

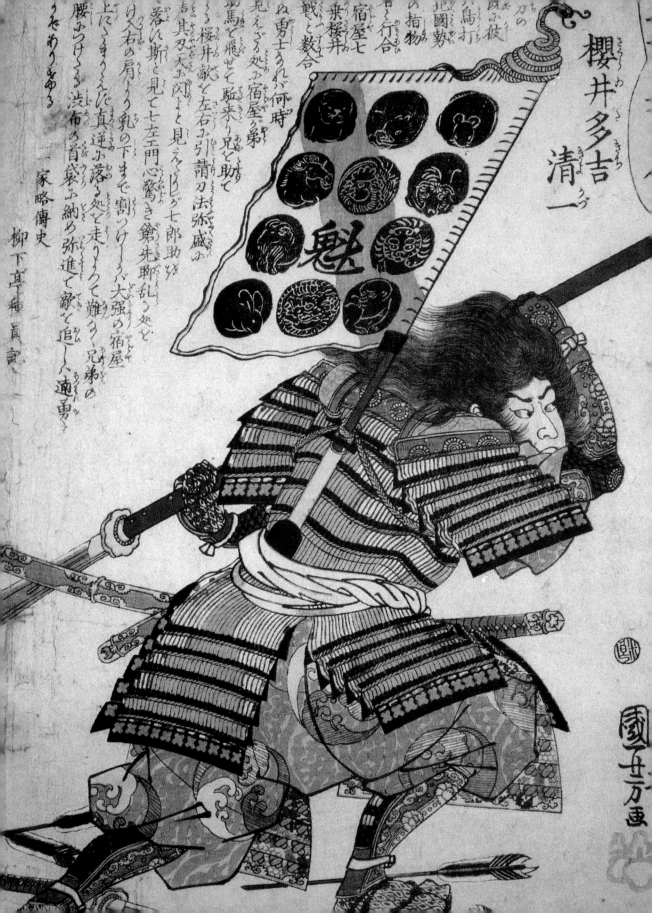

The paradox of tranquillity

This print by Kuniyoshi shows a samurai in battle. He is identified as Sakurai Kiyokazu. He is making great slashing strokes with his *naginata*. His *sashimono* (back flag) is adorned with ornamented black discs surrounding the character for 'leader', in the sense of 'he who leads the way into battle' – a common samurai obsession.

High up in the warm hills of Kagoshima prefecture, the former province of Satsuma, lies the town of Chiran. It is very isolated and difficult to reach by public transport, but few towns in Japan are so rewarding to visit for someone who wishes to touch the heart of the world of the samurai. Little Chiran was part of the Satsuma *han* of the Shimazu family, and contains a number of historical sites that illustrate the themes covered in the previous chapters, even though its charms are not apparent at first sight. There is no magnificent castle as at Himeji. Instead a lonely and overgrown green mound testifies to the 'one province – one castle' policy of Tokugawa Ieyasu. In common with all the other *daimyo*, the Shimazu demonstrated their loyalty to the new shogun by the demolition of Chiran castle and a concentration of resources at the provincial castle of Tsurumaru in Kagoshima city.

The independence enjoyed by successive *daimyo* of Satsuma has been noted on several occasions in this book. They may have slighted their minor castles, but their geographical remoteness meant that the Shimazu did not entirely comply with another of the restrictions placed upon them by the Tokugawa *bakufu*. This was the strict separation between samurai and farmers, a principle set in motion by Hideyoshi's Sword Hunt, placed into law by his Separation Edict, and then transformed into a fact of sociology by the Tokugawa. The idea was that samurai would do nothing but fight, for which they received a stipend. But two and a half centuries of peace, during which they were required to keep

The cultured side of the samurai warrior is neatly illustrated by this hanging scroll, painted by a *daimyo*. It depicts a samurai and the inscription identifies the subject as a member of the Fujiwara family.

themselves in fighting readiness in a world of rising prices, caused severe economic problems for the samurai class throughout Japan. There are tales of samurai pawning their swords and engaging in covert mercantile operations, all the while maintaining the outward appearance of a military elite.

The Shimazu of Satsuma were more open than most about acknowledging the problem, and one way by which they resolved it was to allow their vassals, the Sata family from Chiran, to take up tea cultivation. The venture proved a great success, and the financial results of their enterprise may be seen in the houses and gardens that the Chiran tea growers left behind. The gardens of Chiran, most of which date from the mid- to late 18th century, lie inside stone walls topped by thick, clipped hedges. The walls were originally designed with defensive purposes in mind, as were the stone barricades at the entrances that would stop an enemy charging through the gateway. A toilet was also built near the gate, ostensibly for the convenience of the guests, but also so that the master could eavesdrop on conversations outside. The gardens themselves are reminiscent of the courtyard gardens of Kyôtô, and several of them make use of 'borrowed scenery' from the mountains beyond. Much use is made of clipped azalea bushes and large irregular stones.

Just as Chiran was the little brother to Kagoshima, so each garden is an echo in miniature of the magnificent garden of the Shimazu *daimyo* that lies in the *han* capital itself. This garden, the Iso Tei-en, and the villa that lies beside it, was created for the Shimazu family after Tsurumaru castle was all but destroyed in the Satsuma Rebellion. But where the gardens of Chiran borrow their scenery from the hills beyond, the Iso Tei-en goes one better and uses the spectacular view of the volcano of Sakurajima, sitting out there in the middle of the bay. In another interesting juxtaposition, next door to the Iso Tei-en stands Japan's first Western-style factory, built by Shimazu Nariakira on the advice of Saigô Takamori. This stone building, dating from 1855, helped to create some of Japan's earliest modern armaments. It is now a museum, and among the items on display is one of the original cannon called *kunikuzushi*, the weapon of mass destruction used by the Otomo against the Shimazu so many years before.

There are no cannon factories in the old samurai quarter of Chiran, which represents the peaceful days of the Tokugawa regime. But on leaving the old street of perfect little gardens and crossing the main road that runs parallel to it, one is suddenly reminded of the upheavals of the Meiji Restoration. It is quite a shock, because the visitor is first confronted by one of the oddest tourist attractions in Japan. It is a red double-decker London bus (a number 37 to be precise), and it welcomes visitors to a museum that commemorates the brief period in 1863 when Great Britain and Japan were at war.

The incident came about as a result of the one requirement of the Tokugawa *bakufu* from which the *daimyo* of Satsuma was never able to wriggle free. This was the Alternate Attendance System. The 1863 affair began when some English visitors to

OVERLEAF During the Tokugawa Period the Shimazu of Satsuma allowed their vassals, the Sata family from Chiran, to take up tea cultivation. The venture proved to be a great success, and the financial results of their enterprise may be seen in the houses and gardens they left behind. The gardens of Chiran, most of which date from the mid- to late 18th century, lie inside stone walls topped by thick, clipped hedges. The gardens themselves are reminiscent of the courtyard gardens of Kyôtô, and several of them make use of 'borrowed scenery' from the mountains beyond. This is the garden of Hirayama Soyo.

Japan were out riding, and came upon the procession of the samurai of the Satsuma *daimyo* who were off on their long and complex journey to pay their respects to the shogun. The haughty foreigners refused to dismount when the armed column came by, and one of the Shimazu samurai was so outraged that he drew his sword. A scuffle ensued, during which an Englishman was killed. The outrage this caused was enormous, and compensation was demanded by Great Britain from the Satsuma *han* and also from the *bakufu*, with whom lay the ultimate responsibility for foreign relations. The shogun paid up, but the Shimazu *daimyo* consistently refused to hand over his share of the money, so in August 1863 the Royal Navy bombarded Kagoshima. The London bus marks the entrance to a small museum commemorating the event.

For the final sight on the tourist itinerary of Chiran the visitor has to abandon the tranquillity of the gardens and the curiosity of the London bus for something much darker. A couple of miles from the town centre lies the site of an old military airfield that was established in 1942. At first it was a training camp, but from 1944 onwards Chiran became one of the main centres on the Japanese mainland for the desperate operations that we know as *kamikaze*. In the final flourish of the tradition of the samurai way of death, young pilots were trained at Chiran before they took off for their suicide missions. With a samurai headband tied around their foreheads they piloted their cramped and doomed aircraft on their one-way journeys. The men were immersed in evocative names from the warriors' past that linked the *kamikaze* squadrons and their weapons to the world of the warrior. There was 'cherry blossom' – the eternal symbol of the fallen hero. There was also the 'chrysanthemum on the water' – the device that appeared on the flag of Kusunoki Masashige to show how the loyal Kusunoki sustained the true emperor of the Southern Court.

The old airfield is now a museum with the politically correct title of the 'Special Attack Force Peace Hall'. Its memorabilia, which include salvaged remains of *kamikaze* planes that had just missed their target and photographs of the young pilots, make no reference to the earlier samurai tradition that required just such a

ABOVE These remains of a Zero fighter used as a *kamikaze* suicide plane are on display at Chiran. The *kamikaze* pilots took their name from the 'divine tempest' that destroyed the invading Mongol fleet in 1281.

RIGHT This statue of a *kamikaze* pilot stands outside the museum dedicated to the *kamikaze* pilots at Chiran in Kagoshima prefecture. Chiran was one of the main bases from where suicide attacks were planned and launched.

sacrifice on the field of Kawanakajima. Also, there is no display about the other role that was played by the base at Chiran. Only a very small proportion out of the large number of *kamikaze* planes that set off ever reached their targets to complete their missions. Many were shot down, or crashed, or suffered engine failure, but there were a few examples where the engine that failed lay in the mind of the pilot. Broken in spirit, these men turned back, and landed their planes safely knowing the disgrace that awaited them. The experience of the Hôjô retainers in the cave at Kamakura and the White Tigers on the hill of Iimori was not for them. There was to be no shrine at Chiran in their memory. Instead an obscure corner of the airfield became their prison.

It is a long walk from the peaceful gardens of Chiran to the air-conditioned chill of the Peace Museum. It is an even longer

journey in terms of concept, a distance that takes one from cherry blossom as flower to cherry blossom as symbol. It encompasses the spectrum from detachment as an aesthetic value to detachment from life itself. What unites both extremes is the tremendous paradox that lies at the heart of the world of the samurai. This is the paradox of tranquillity, where one concept fulfils two very different roles. The first situation is that of finding a peace outside oneself in the contemplation of the harmonious arrangement of stones and shrubs, balanced and framed beyond by distant scenery. The unique Japanese mystery is the transference of that same tranquillity to the moment of death, whether that death was brought about by a cold blade or a roaring metal tomb of high explosive. 'The way of the samurai', wrote the author of *Hagakure*, 'is to be found in death.' In Chiran that whole world of the warrior is still to be found, lying in deep repose.

Glossary

ashigaru	footsoldier, from about 1590, the lowest-ranking samurai
bakufu	the government of the shogun
biwa	the Japanese lute
bushido	'the way of the warrior'
byobu	folding screen
daimyo	feudal lord of a Japanese province
emishi	the indigenous tribes of Japan
furangi	breech-loading cannon
gyorin	Battle formation; intended to make an army appear as if it were preparing to retreat-thereby tricking an enemy into attacking.
han	the territory ruled by a daimyo under the Tokugawa
haniwa	primitive but lifelike clay models of soldiers
hara kiri	*see* seppuku
honjo	a daimyo's headquarters castle
junshi	following a lord in death by suicide
kaishaku	a 'second' during seppuku
kami	Shintô god or deity
kamikaze	'the divine wind', the typhoon that destroyed the Mongol fleet in 1281; the term also refers to the suicide pilots of World War II
kanshi	suicide as a protest
kofun	the large earthwork tombs of the Yamato rulers of ancient Japan

koguchi	tigers' mouth
Kuwagata	horns
maku	curtains that surrounded a general's headquarters on a battlefield
mon	a family badge
naginata	a halberd, or spear with a curved blade
nobori	a long vertical banner
sake	rice wine
samurai	a member of the warrior class of Japan
sashimono	the identifying flag worn on the back of samurai armour
seppuku	the act of suicide by disembowelment
shikken	the regency of the Hôjô family
shogun	the military dictator of Japan
sokotsu-shi	expiatory suicide
tsunami	freak wave
tatami	floor mat
uji	the ancient clans of Japan
wako	Japanese pirates
wajo	the Japanese coastal forts in Korea
yabusame	the martial art of mounted archery
yamashiro	a mountain-top castle

Bibliography

Asakawa, K., *The Documents of Iriki: Illustrative of the Development of the Feudal Institutions of Japan*, Greenwood, Westport, Conn., 1929 (reprinted 1974).

Aston, W. G., *Nihongi: Chronicles of Japan from the Earliest Times to AD 697*, Tuttle and Co., Vermont, 1972.

Ballard, G. A., *The Influence of the Sea on the Political History of Japan*, John Murray, London, 1921.

Barker, A. J., *Suicide Weapon*, Pan Ballantine, London, 1971.

Beasley, W. G., *The Meiji Restoration*, Stanford University Press, 1973.

Berry, Mary E., *Hideyoshi*, Harvard University Press, 1982.

Bonar, H. A. C., 'On Maritime Enterprise in Japan', *Transactions of the Asiatic Society of Japan*, 15, pp. 103–23, 1887.

Boscaro, A., *101 Letters of Hideyoshi*, Sophia University, Tokyo, 1975.

Boxer, C. R., 'Notes on early military influence on Japan', *Transactions of the Asiatic Society of Japan* (2nd series), 8, pp. 68–95, 1931.

Boxer, C. R., *The Christian Century in Japan 1549–1650*, University of California Press, Berkeley, 1951.

Cortazzi, Hugh, *Dr Willis in Japan: British Medical Pioneer, 1862–1877*, Athlone Press, London, 1985.

Covell, J. C., and Covell, A., *Korean Impact on Japanese Culture: Japan's Hidden History*, Hollym, Elizabeth, NJ, 1984.

Craig, Albert M., *Chôshû in the Meiji Restoration*, Harvard University Press, 1961.

Hall, J. W. (ed.) *The Cambridge History of Japan: Volume 4, Early Modern Japan*, Cambridge University Press, 1991.

Hazard, Benjamin H., 'The Formative Years of the Wako, 1223–63', *Monumenta Nipponica*, xxii, 3, 4, pp. 260–77, 1967.

Hazard, Benjamin H., *Japanese Marauding in Medieval Korea: The Wako Impact on Late Koryo*, Unpublished PhD Thesis, University of California, Berkeley, 1967.

Ikegami, Eiko, *The Taming of the Samurai: Honorific Individualism and the Making of Modern Japan*, Harvard University Press, 1994.

Kitagawa, Hiroshi and Tsuchida, Bruce, *The Tale of Heike (Heike Monogatari)*, University of Tokyo Press, 1975.

Kuno Y. S., *Japanese Expansion on the Asiatic Continent*, University of California Press, Berkeley, 1937.

Mahito, Ishimitsu (ed.), *Remembering Aizu: The Testament of Shiba Goro*, translated with notes by Teruko Craig, University of Hawaii Press, Honolulu, 1999.

Masuda, Wataru, *Japan and China: Mutual Representations in the Modern Era*, translated by Joshua A. Fogel, Curzon Press, 2000.

McCullough, Helen, *The Taiheiki: A Chronicle of Medieval Japan*, Columbia University Press, New York, 1959.

Morris, Ivan, *The Nobility of Failure: Tragic Heroes in the History of Japan*, Secker and Warburg, London, 1975.

Philippi, Donald L., *Kojiki*, translated with an introduction and notes, University of Tokyo Press, 1969.

Sadler, A. L., *The Maker of Modern Japan: The Life of Tokugawa Ieyasu*, Allen and Unwin, London, 1937.

Sadler, A. L., 'The Naval Campaign in the Korean War of Hideyoshi', *Transactions of the Asiatic Society of Japan* (2nd series), 14, pp.179–208, 1937.

Seward, Jack, *Hara-kiri: Japanese Ritual Suicide*, Tuttle, Vermont, 1968.

Smith R. D., 'Towards a new typology for wrought iron ordnance', *The International Journal of Nautical Archaeology and Underwater Exploration*, 17, 1, pp. 5–16, 1988.

Takahashi, K., *Hata Sashimono*, Akida Shoten, Tokyo, 1965.

Takekoshi, Yosaburo, *The Economic Aspects of the History of the Civilisation of Japan*, London, 1930.

Takegoshi, Y., *The Story of the Wako*, translated by Hideo Watanabe Kenkyusha, Tokyo, 1940.

Takenouchi, Kazusai, *Ehon Taikoki* (Woodblock printed edition, Kobayashi Rokubei, Osaka, 1802); (Printed edition, Yuhodo Bunko Series, no. 81, 1917)

Tanaka Taneo, 'Japan's Relations with Overseas Countries' in Hall and Toyoda (eds), *Japan in the Muromachi Age*, University of California Press, pp. 159–78), 1977.

Tsunoda, R., de Bary, W., and Keene, D. (eds), *Sources of Japanese Tradition Volume I*, Columbia University Press, 1958.

Varley, Paul, *Warriors of Japan as Portrayed in the War Tales*, University of Hawaii Press, 1994.

Wilson, William R., *Hôgen Monogatari*, Sophia University Press, Tokyo, 1971.

Yamaguchi, Kohei, *Byakkotai*, Aizu-Wakamatsu City, 1948.

Yamamoto Tsunetomo, *Hagakure The Book of the Samurai*, translated by William Scott Wilson, Kodansha, Tokyo, 1979.

Index